A SEASON IN HELL
and
ILLUMINATIONS

T0151852

A SEASON IN HELL
AND
ILLUMINATIONS

Poems by Arthur Rimbaud

Translated by Bertrand Mathieu

Pen and Ink Drawings by Denzil Walker

BOA Edtitions, Ltd. • Rochester, NY

09 10 11   14 13 12

LC # : 91-73275

The publication of this book was made possible with the assistance of grants from
the Sonia Raiziss Giop Charitable Foundation,
The Literature Program of the New York State Council on the Arts, and the
Literature Program of the National Endowment for the Arts.
BOA Editions, Ltd., is a not-for-profit corporation under section 501 (c) (3)
of the United States Internal Revenue Code.

Typesetting: The Typeworks
Manufacturing: McNaughton & Gunn

Cover Art: Denzil Walker
Cover Design: Daphne Poulin
BOA Logo: Mirko

BOA Editions, Ltd.
Nora A. Jones, Executive Director/Publisher
Thom Ward, Editor/Production
Peter Conners, Editor/Marketing
Bernadette Catalana, BOA Board Chair
A. Poulin, Jr., Founder (1938-1996)
250 North Goodman Street, Suite 306
Rochester, NY 14607
www.boaeditions.org

These new American translations
of Rimbaud's two major works
are for my brother
DONALD MATHIEU

TABLE DE MATÌERES

TABLE OF CONTENTS

A SEASON IN HELL

— 1 —

Rimbaud finished writing *A Season in Hell* in the summer of 1873, in a dilapidated barn behind the farmhouse of his unbelievably harsh and miserly mother, in the hamlet of Roche, near the French town of Charleville on the Belgian border. Ever since, the majority of Rimbaud's readers and critics have thought of this tormented work of genius as Rimbaud's "farewell to literature." We now know with absolute certainty—thanks to the researches of Etiemble, Wallace Fowlie, Enid Starkie, Yves Bonnefoy, and Alain Borer—that this is not true. Most of the poems in *Illuminations* were written after *A Season in Hell*. And there is scant but intriguing evidence that Rimbaud may have written other long poems during his seventeen years of supposed "silence" in Africa—poems as yet unknown to us, poems waiting impatiently to be discovered in some attic or warehouse, *some*where. *A Season in Hell* is not the story of a man who is giving up. It's the story of an extraordinarily gifted artist who is in the process of discovering, in great pain and amazement, the inextinguishable powers of his own voice.

— 2 —

A Season in Hell is a terribly enigmatic poem, but it's not an entirely hermetic one. I believe there is some merit to thinking of it as a kind of psychodrama. The stage is the poet's brain. The play is poetry-in-the-making, soul-in-the-making. The dual characters adopt a variety of shifting shapes throughout, but they are easy enough to recognize and understand: angel/demon, heaven/hell, happiness/misery, good/evil, bride/bridegroom. To put it in simpler terms, *Yin/Yang*. Actually, *A Season in Hell* is a brilliantly near-hysterical quarrel between the poet and his "other." Here's a passage from Rimbaud's letter of May 15, 1871, to Paul Demeny:" *I* is someone else. If the brass wakes up a trumpet, it's not its own fault. *This* is obvious to me: I assist at the birth of my thought: I watch it and listen to it: I draw a stroke of the bow: the symphony makes a stir in the depths, or leaps at a bound on the stage." The two voices heard in *Season* are the two separate parts of Rimbaud's schizoid personality—the "I" who is a seer/poet and the "I" who is the incredibly hardnosed Widow Rimbaud's peasant/son. One voice is wildly in love with the miracle of light and childhood, the other finds all these literary shenanigans rather damnable and "idiotic."

—3—

Wallace Fowlie calls *A Season in Hell* "a kind of morality play where reminiscences immediate and distant are juxtaposed with impulses to rebellion and outbursts of exuberance." (Wallace Fowlie, *Climate of Violence,* Macmillan, 1967.) This description is absolutely flawless, but it still leaves us with an essential problem. What does such a poem have to *give* us? The trouble with *A Season in Hell* is that it points only one way: where it's going is where it's coming from. Its greatest source of frustration, like that of every important poem, is the realization that it's impossible for any of us to escape the set limits imposed on us by "reality." "We can't *take off*," Rimbaud says at one of the most heart-breaking moments in the poem—unless we discover the trick of combining "one soul with one body." The "way out" is the open road to the Absolute, a road shunned by practical-minded men and women because it's a road full of risks. Only the true absolutists of the imagination keep coming back to it, again and again, because they alone know it's the only road that can actually reach heaven. The French poet Pierre Reverdy, one of Rimbaud's boldest disciples, speaks of these absolutists as

Those who are the butts of ridicule
Those who carry inside them the drop of eternity necessary to life
Those who've never recognized their own limitations

Whenever they travel on the road that's bounded up by heaven
    alone
And bend their heads a bit
Stars get all tangled up in their hair.

—4—

Jean Cocteau used to say: "Qui gagne perd, qui perd gagne." Rimbaud is a poet who was bent on losing in order to gain everything. Only total revolt against the trivializing tendencies of "everyday life" can yield a solid measure of light. Only a terribly intimate familiarity with Nothingness—the most brutal and most blissful of all the angels—

can release the mysteriously cunning word that will make things happen, that will "change life." This word, it seems to me, is waiting in *A Season in Hell*, somewhere. We may not know what to make of the shrieks of pain and the tortured rhetoric and the broken wings, but we know beyond a doubt that Icarus sees something incredible and marvelous before he falls into the sea and vanishes.

— BERTRAND MATHIEU

Jadis, si je me souviens bien, ma vie était un festin où s'ouvraient tous les coeurs, où tous les vins coulaient.

Un soir, j'ai assis la Beauté sur mes genoux.—Et je l'ai trouvée amère.—Et je l'ai injuriée.

Je me suis armé contre la justice.

Je me suis enfui. Ô sorcières, ô misère, ô haine, c'est à vous que mon trésor a été confié!

Je parvins à faire s'évanouir dans mon esprit toute l'espérance humaine. Sur toute joie pour l'étrangler j'ai fait le bond sourd de la bête féroce.

J'ai appelé les bourreaux pour, en périssant, mordre la crosse de leurs fusils. J'ai appelé les fléaux, pour m'étouffer avec le sable, le sang. Le malheur a été mon dieu. Je me suis allongé dans la boue. Je me suis séché à l'air du crime. Et j'ai joué de bons tours à la folie.

Et le printemps m'a apporté l'affreux rire de l'idiot.

Or, tout dernièrement m'étant trouvé sur le point de faire le dernier *couac!* j'ai songé à rechercher la clef du festin ancien, où je reprendrais peut-être appétit.

La charité est cette clef.—Cette inspiration prouve que j'ai rêvé!

«Tu resteras hyène, etc... », se récrie le démon qui me couronna de si aimables pavots. «Gagne la mort avec tous tes appétits, et ton égoïsme et tous les péchés capitaux.»

Ah! j'en ai trop pris:—Mais, cher Satan, je vous en conjure, une prunelle moins irritée! et en attendant les quelques petites lâchetés en retard, vous qui aimez dans l'écrivain l'absence des facultés descriptives ou instructives, je vous détache ces quelques hideux feuillets de mon carnet de damné.

A while back, if I remember right, my life was one long party where all hearts were open wide, where all wines kept flowing.

One night, I sat Beauty down on my lap.—And I found her galling.—And I roughed her up.

I armed myself against justice.

I ran away. O witches, O misery, O hatred, my treasure's been turned over to you!

I managed to make every trace of human hope vanish from my mind. I pounced on every joy like a ferocious animal eager to strangle it.

I called for executioners so that, while dying, I could bite the butts of their rifles. I called for plagues to choke me with sand, with blood. Bad luck was my god. I stretched out in the muck. I dried myself in the air of crime. And I played tricks on insanity.

And Spring brought me the frightening laugh of the idiot.

So, just recently, when I found myself on the brink of the final *squawk!*, it dawned on me to look again for the key to that ancient party where I might find my appetite once more.

Charity is that key.—This inspiration proves I was dreaming!

"You'll always be a hyena etc...," yells the devil, who'd crowned me with such pretty poppies. "Deserve death with all your appetites, your selfishness, and all the capital sins!"

Ah! I've been through too much:—But, sweet Satan, I beg of you, a less blazing eye! and while waiting for the new little cowardly gestures yet to come, since you like an absence of descriptive or didactic skills in a writer, let me rip out these few ghastly pages from my notebook of the damned.

J'ai de mes ancêtres gaulois l'oeil bleu blanc, la cervelle étroite, et la maladresse dans la lutte. Je trouve mon habillement aussi barbare que le leur. Mais je ne beurre pas ma chevelure.

Les Gaulois étaient les écorcheurs de bêtes, les brûleurs d'herbes les plus ineptes de leur temps.

D'eux j'ai: l'idolâtrie et l'amour du sacrilège;—oh! tous les vices, colère, luxure,—magnifique, la luxure;—surtout mensonge et paresse.

J'ai horreur de tous les métiers. Maîtres et ouvriers, tous paysans, ignobles. La main à plume vaut la maïn à charrue.—Quel siècle à mains!—Je n'aurai jamais ma main. Après, la domesticité mène trop loin. L'honnêteté de la mendicité me navre. Les criminels dégoûtent comme des châtrés: moi, je suis intact, et ça m'est égal.

Mais! qui a fait ma langue perfide tellement, qu'elle ait guidé et sauvegardé jusqu'ici ma paresse? Sans me servir pour vivre même de mon corps, et plus oisif que le crapaud, j'ai vécu partout. Pas une famille d'Europe que je ne connaisse.—J'entends des familles comme la mienne, qui tiennent tout de la déclaration des Droits de l'Homme.—J'ai connu chaque fils de famille!

———————

Si j'avais des antécédents à un point quelconque de l'histoire de France!

Mais non, rien.

Il m'est bien évident que j'ai toujours été race inférieure. Je ne puis comprendre la révolte. Ma race ne se souleva jamais que pour piller: tels les loups à la bête qu'ils n'ont pas tuée.

Je me rappelle l'histoire de la France fille aînée de l'Église. J'aurais fait, manant, le voyage de terre sainte; j'ai dans la tête des routes dans les plaines souabes, des vues de Byzance, des remparts de Solyme; le culte de Marie, l'attendrissement sur le crucifié s'éveillent en moi parmi mille féeries profanes.—Je suis assis, lépreux, sur les pots cassés et les orties, au pied d'un mur rongé par le soleil.—Plus tard, reître, j'aurais bivaqué sous les nuits d'Allemagne.

Ah! encore: je danse le sabbat dans une rouge clairière, avec des vieilles et des enfants.

I've got my Gallic ancestors' light-blue eyes, their narrow skull, and their clumsiness in combat. I consider my clothes as barbaric as theirs. Only, I don't butter my hair.

The Gauls were the most inept skinners of beasts and scorchers of grass of their time.

From them I get: idolatry and the love of sacrilege—oh! all the vices, anger, lust—magnificent, this lust—especially lying and laziness.

I despise all trades. Foremen and workmen—all of them, peasants, riff-raff. The hand that writes is as good as the hand that ploughs.— What a century of hands!—I'll never own my hand. Next, domesticity goes too far. The honesty of begging sickens me. Criminals are as disgusting as castrati. Myself, I'm intact, and I don't give a damn.

But! who made my tongue so tricky that it's managed to guide and guard my laziness up till now? Without even using my body for a living, and loafing around more than a toad, I've lived everywhere. Not a family in Europe that I don't know.—I mean families like my own which owe everything to the Declaration of the Rights of Man.—I've known every mother's son of such families.

If only I had ancestors at some point in French history!

But no, nothing.

It's very obvious to me I've always belonged to an inferior race. I can't understand revolt. My race never rose up except to loot: like wolves after beasts they haven't killed.

I recall the history of France, the Church's eldest daughter. Once, as a serf, I made the journey to the Holy Land. My head's full of roads through the Swabian plains, views of Byzantium, ramparts of Jerusalem: the cult of Mary, compassion for the Crucified One wake up in me among a thousand profane fantasies.—I'm sitting there, a leper, among smashed vases and nettles, at the foot of a wall gnawed by the sun.— Later on, a trooper, it seems I bivouacked under German stars.

Ah, once again! I'm dancing the witches' sabbath in a reddish clearing with old women and children.

Je ne me souviens pas plus loin que cette terre-ci et le christianisme. Je n'en finirais pas de me revoir dans ce passé. Mais toujours seul; sans famille; même, quelle langue parlais-je? Je ne me vois jamais dans les conseils du Christ; ni dans les conseils des Seigneurs,—représentants du Christ.

Qu'étais-je au siècle dernier: je ne me retrouve qu'aujourd'hui. Plus de vagabonds, plus de guerres vagues. La race inférieure a tout couvert—le peuple, comme on dit, la raison; la nation et la science.

Oh! la science! On a tout repris. Pour le corps et pour l'âme,—le viatique,—on a la médecine et la philosophie,—les remèdes de bonnes femmes et les chansons populaires arrangées. Et les divertissements des princes et les jeux qu'ils interdisaient! Géographie, cosmographie, mécanique, chimie!...

La science, la nouvelle noblesse! Le progrès. Le monde marche! Pourquoi ne tournerait-il pas?

C'est la vision des nombres. Nous allons à l'*Esprit*. C'est très-certain, c'est oracle, ce que je dis. Je comprends, et ne sachant m'expliquer sans paroles païennes, je voudrais me taire.

———————

Le sang païen revient! L'Esprit est proche, pourquoi Christ ne m'aide-t-il pas, en donnant à mon âme noblesse et liberté. Hélas! l'Évangile a passé! l'Évangile! l'Évangile.

J'attends Dieu avec gourmandise. Je suis de race inférieure de toute éternité.

Me voici sur la plage armoricaine. Que les villes s'allument dans le soir. Ma journée est faite; je quitte l'Europe. L'air marin brûlera mes poumons; les climats perdus me tanneront. Nager, broyer l'herbe, chasser, fumer surtout; boire des liqueurs fortes comme du métal bouillant,—comme faisaient ces chers ancêtres autour des feux.

Je reviendrai, avec des membres de fer, la peau sombre, l'oeil furieux: sur mon masque, on me jugera d'une race forte. J'aurai de l'or: je serai oisif et brutal. Les femmes soignent ces féroces infirmes retour des pays chauds. Je serai mêlé aux affaires politiques. Sauvé.

Maintenant je suis maudit, j'ai horreur de la patrie. Le meilleur, c'est un sommeil bien ivre, sur la grève.

———————

I can't remember farther back than this very earth and Christianity. I'll never stop seeing myself in that past. But always alone. Without family. Still, what language did I speak? I never see myself in the councils of Christ. Nor in the councils of the Nobility—the representatives of Christ.

What was I in the last century? Only today do I find traces of myself. No more vagabonds, no more vague wars. The inferior race has covered everything—the people, as we say, reason, the nation and science.

O science! Everything's been taken care of. For the body and soul— the last rites—there's medicine and there's philosophy—old wives' remedies and new arrangements of popular songs. And the pastimes of princes and the games they've outlawed! Geography, cosmography, mechanics, chemistry . . . !

Science, the new nobility! Progress. The world moves ahead! Why shouldn't it turn?

It's the vision of numbers. We're going towards the *spirit*. What I'm saying is absolutely sure, it's oracular. I understand and, not knowing how to explain myself without using pagan words, I'd rather shut up.

Pagan blood comes again! the Spirit is near. Why doesn't Christ help me by giving my soul nobility and liberty! Too bad, the gospel's *passé!* the Gospel! the Gospel.

I wait for God with gluttony. I belong to an inferior race throughout eternity.

Here I am on the Brittany beach. Let the cities light up in the evening. My own day is done. I'm quitting Europe. Sea air will burn my lungs. Lost climates will tan my hide. I'll swim, I'll trample the grass, hunt, smoke especially. I'll drink liquor hard as boiling metal—like my dear old ancestors around their fires.

I'll come back with limbs of iron, skin darkened, a furious eye. Seeing my mask, they'll think I'm from a tough race. I'll have gold: I'll be lazy and brutal. Women love to nurse fierce invalids who come back from hot countries. I'll get mixed up in politics. Saved.

Right now I'm an outcast, I loathe the homeland. The best thing for me's a boozy nap on the beach.

On ne part pas.—Reprenons les chemins d'ici, chargé de mon vice, le vice qui a poussé ses racines de souffrance à mon côté, dès l'âge de raison—qui monte au ciel, me bat, me renverse, me traîne.

La dernière innocence et la dernière timidité. C'est dit. Ne pas porter au monde mes dégoûts et mes trahisons.

Allons! La marche, le fardeau, le désert, l'ennui et la colère.

À qui me louer? Quelle bête faut-il adorer? Quelle sainte image attaque-t-on? Quels coeurs briserai-je? Quel mensonge dois-je tenir?—Dans quel sang marcher?

Plutôt, se garder de la justice.—La vie dure, l'abrutissement simple,—soulever, le poing desséché, le couvercle du cercueil, s'asseoir, s'étouffer. ainsi point de vieillesse, ni de dangers: la terreur n'est pas française.

—Ah! je suis tellement délaissé que j'offre à n'importe quelle divine image des élans vers la perfection.

Ô mon abnégation, ô ma charité merveilleuse! ici-bas, pourtant!

De *profundis Domine,* suis-je bête!

Encore tout enfant, j'admirais le forçat intraitable sur qui se referme toujours le bagne; je visitais les auberges et les garnis qu'il aurait sacrés par son séjour; je voyais *avec son idée* le ciel bleu et le travail fleuri de la campagne; je flairais sa fatalité dans les villes. Il avait plus de force qu'un saint, plus de bon sens qu'un voyageur—et lui, lui seul! pour témoin de sa gloire et de sa raison.

Sur les routes, par des nuits d'hiver, sans gîte, sans habits, sans pain, une voix étreignait mon coeur gelé: «Faiblesse ou force: te voilà, c'est la force. Tu ne sais ni où tu vas ni pourquoi tu vas, entre partout, réponds à tout. On ne te tuera pas plus que si tu étais cadavre.» Au matin j'avais le regard si perdu et la contenance si morte, que ceux que j'ai rencontrés *ne m'ont peut-être pas vu.*

Dans les villes la boue m'apparaissait soudainement rouge et noire, comme une glace quand la lampe circule dans la chambre voisine, comme un trésor dans la forêt! Bonne chance, criais-je, et je voyais une mer de flammes et de fumée au ciel; et, à gauche, à droite, toutes les richesses flambant comme un milliard de tonnerres.

We can't take off.—Back again to local roads, lugging my vice, the vice that's grown its roots of suffering at my side since the age of reason—that rises to the skies, clobbers me, knocks me down, drags me along.

The ultimate innocence and the ultimate shyness. So they say. Never to show the world my disgusts and my betrayals.

Let's go! The march, the burden, the desert, the boredom, and the rage.

Who needs a hired hand? Which beast do I worship? Which holy icon do we attack? Whose hearts do I break? What lie do I cling to?—In what blood do I stomp?

Instead, steer clear of justice.—The rugged life, uncomplicated brutishness—just lift the coffin's lid with a withered fist, sit down, suffocate. This way no old age, no dangers: terror isn't French.

—Ah! I feel so godforsaken that I offer my yearnings for perfection to any divine image whatsoever.

O my abnegation, O my marvelous charity! but here on earth!

De profundis, Domine . . . what a jackass I am!

When I was still a child, I admired the intractable convict the prison gates were closed on forever. I visited the taverns and rooming houses he'd consecrated by his stay. I looked at the blue sky and the flower-patterns in the countryside *with his mind.* I could smell his downfall in the cities. He had more strength than a saint, more horse sense than a traveler—and he, he alone! as a witness of his reknown and his rightness.

On the roads on winter nights, with no roof, no clothes, no bread, a voice clutched at my heart: "Weakness or strength: there you are, it's strength. You don't know where you're going, or why you're going. Go everywhere, answer everything. They won't kill you any more than they'd kill a corpse." In the morning I'd have a look so lost and features so dead that people I met *probably didn't see me.*

In the cities the mud suddenly seemed to me reddish and black, like a mirror when the lamp moves around in the next room, like a treasure in the woods! Good luck, I shouted, and I saw a sea of flames and smoke in the sky. And on the left and right, all sorts of fabulous riches blazed like a billion thunderbolts.

Mais l'orgie et la camaraderie des femmes m'étaient interdites. Pas même un compagnon. Je me voyais devant une foule exaspérée, en face du peloton d'exécution, pleurant du malheur qu'ils n'aient pu comprendre, et pardonnant!—Comme Jeanne d'Arc!—«Prêtres, professeurs, maîtres, vous vous trompez en me livrant à la justice. Je n'ai jamais été de ce peuple-ci; je n'ai jamais été chrétien; je suis de la race qui chantait dans le supplice; je ne comprends pas les lois; je n'ai pas le sens moral, je suis une brute: vous vous trompez... »

Oui, j'ai les yeux fermés à votre lumière. Je suis une bête, un nègre. Mais je puis être sauvé. vous êtes de faux nègres, vous maniaques, féroces, avares. Marchand, tu es nègre; magistrat, tu es nègre; général, tu es nègre; empereur, vieille démangeaison, tu es nègre: tu as bu d'une liqueur non taxée, de la fabrique de Satan.—Ce peuple est inspiré par la fièvre et le cancer. Infirmes et vieillards sont tellement respectables qu'ils demandent à être bouillis.—Le plus malin est de quitter ce continent, où la folie rôde pour pourvoir d'otages ces misérables. J'entre au vrai royaume des enfants de Cham.

Connais-je encore la nature? me connais-je?—*Plus de mots.* J'ensevelis les morts dans mon ventre. Cris, tambour, danse, danse, danse, danse! Je ne vois même pas l'heure où, les blancs débarquant, je tomberai au néant.

Faim, soif, cris, danse, danse, danse, danse!

Les blancs débarquent. Le canon! Il faut se soumettre au baptême, s'habiller, travailler.

J'ai reçu au coeur le coup de la grâce. ah! je ne l'avais pas prévu!

Je n'ai point fait le mal. Les jours vont m'être légers, le repentir me sera épargné. Je n'aurai pas eu les tourments de l'âme presque morte au bien, où remonte la lumière sévère comme les cierges funéraires. Le sort du fils de famille, cercueil prématuré couvert de limpides larmes. Sans doute la débauche est bête, le vice est bête; il faut jeter la pourriture à l'écart. Mais l'horloge ne sera pas arrivée à ne plus sonner que l'heure de la pure douleur! Vais-je être enlevé comme un enfant, pour jouer au paradis dans l'oubli de tout le malheur!

Vite! est-il d'autres vies?—Le sommeil dans la richesse est impossible. La richesse a toujours été bien public. L'amour divin seul octroie les clefs de la science. Je vois que la nature n'est qu'un spectacle de bonté. Adieu chimères, idéals, erreurs.

But orgies and the company of women weren't available to me. Not even a buddy. I could see myself in front of an infuriated mob, facing a firing squad, weeping over the misfortune they couldn't have understood, and forgiving!—Like Joan of Arc!—"Priests, professors, masters, you're making a mistake by turning me over to justice. I've never belonged to this people. I've never been a Christian. I'm of the breed that sang under torture. I don't understand laws. I've got no moral sense, I'm a brute: you're making a mistake...!"

Sure, my eyes are closed to your light. I'm a beast, a nigger. But I can be saved. You're all phoney niggers, you maniacs, zealots, misers. Businessman, you're a nigger. Judge, you're a nigger. General, you're a nigger. Emperor—Old Itchiness—you're a nigger, you've drunk untaxed liquor from Satan's distillery.—These people are uplifted by fever and cancer. Cripples and old people are so respectable, they cry out to be boiled.—The smartest thing would be to get off this continent where insanity prowls around to supply these wretches with hostages. I'm entering the true kingdom of the children of Hām.

Do I know Nature yet? do I know myself?—*No more words.* I bury the dead in my belly. Shouts, drum, dance, dance, dance, dance! I can't even imagine the time when, after the white men have landed, I'll plunge into Nothingness.

Hunger, thirst, shouts, dance, dance, dance, dance!

The white men are landing! The cannon! We've got to submit to baptism, getting dressed, work.

I just got a stroke of grace through the heart. Ah, that I hadn't expected!

I've done no evil. My days will be light, I'll be spared repentence. I won't have known the torments of the soul that's almost dead to goodness, from which a light glows through as grave as funeral candles. The fate of sons of good families: the premature coffin covered with limpid tears. Naturally, debauchery is stupid, vice is stupid. What's rotten's to be swept aside. But the clock won't have managed to strike anything but the hour of pure pain. Am I going to be picked up like a child to play in Paradise and forget everything painful?

Quick! are there other lives?—Sound sleep's impossible for the rich. Wealth has always been public property. Divine love alone confers the keys of knowledge. I see now that Nature's nothing but an extravaganza of goodness. Goodbye chimeras, ideals, errors.

Le chant raisonnable des anges s'élève du navire sauveur: c'est l'amour divin.—Deux amours! je puis mourir de l'amour terrestre, mourir de dévouement. J'ai laissé des âmes dont la peine s'accroîtra de mon départ! vous me choisissez parmi les naufragés; ceux qui restent sont-ils pas mes amis?

Sauvez-les!

La raison m'est née. Le monde st bon. Je bénirai la vie. J'aimerai mes frères. Ce ne sont plus des promesses d'enfance. Ni l'espoir d'échapper à la vieillesse et à la mort. Dieu fait ma force, et je loue Dieu.

———————

L'ennui n'est plus mon amour. Les rages, les débauches, la folie, dont je sais tous les élans et les désastres,—tout mon fardeau est déposé. Apprécions sans vertige l'étendue de mon innocence.

Je ne serais plus capable de demander le réconfort d'une bastonnade. Je ne me crois pas embarqué pour une noce avec Jésus-Christ pour beau-père.

Je ne suis pas prisonnier de ma raison. J'ai dit: Dieu. Je veux la liberté dans le salut: comment la poursuivre? Les goûts frivoles m'ont quitté. Plus besoin de dévouement ni d'amour divin. Je ne regrette pas le siècle des coeurs sensibles. Chacun a sa raison, mépris et charité: je retiens ma place au sommet de cette angélique échelle de bon sens.

Quant au bonheur établi, domestique ou non... non, je ne peux pas. Je suis trop dissipé, trop faible. La vie fleurit par le travail, vieille vérité: moi, ma vie n'est pas assez pesante, elle s'envole et flotte loin au-dessus de l'action, ce cher point du monde.

Comme je deviens vieille fille, à manquer du courage d'aimer la mort!

Si Dieu m'accordait le calme céleste, aérien, la prière,—comme les anciens saints.—Les saints! des forts! les anachorètes, des artistes comme il n'en faut plus!

Farce continuelle! Mon innocence me ferait pleurer. La vie est la farce à mener par tous.

———————

Assez! voici la punition. —*En marche!*

Ah! les poumons brûlent, les tempes grondent! la nuit roule dans mes yeux, par ce soleil! le coeur... les membres...

———————

The reasonable song of angels rises from the rescue ship: it's divine love.—Two loves! I can die of earthly love or die of devotedness. I've cast aside the souls whose pain will increase by my going! Of all the shipwrecked, you're choosing me. Aren't those who are left behind my friends?

Save them!

Reason's born in me. The world is good. I'll start blessing life. I'll love my brothers. These aren't childish promises anymore. Nor the hope of escaping old age and death. God's my strength, and I praise God.

Boredom's no longer my love. Rage, dissipation, insanity—I've known all their excitement and disasters—my whole burden's laid down. Let's coolly consider the extent of my innocence.

I wouldn't be able to ask for the comforts of a thrashing any more. I don't consider myself setting out on a wedding with Jesus Christ as father-in-law.

I'm not a prisoner of my reason. I said: God. I want freedom in salvation—how do I find it? I've lost my taste for the frivolous. No more need of devotion nor of divine love. I don't miss the century of bleeding hearts. Each has its charms, contempt and charity. And I reserve my place at the top of this angelic ladder of good sense.

As for conventional happiness, domestic or not... no, I just can't. I'm too worn out, too weak. Life flourishes only when you work, an old cliché! As for me, my life doesn't weigh enough, it flies off and floats high up above action—that point so dear to the world.

What an old maid I'm getting to be because I lack the courage to fall in love with death!

If only God granted me heavenly aerial calm and prayer—like the ancient saints.—The saints! tough types! anchorites, such artists we don't need any more!

Ceaseless joke! My innocence makes me weep. Life's the joke each of us keeps on playing.

Enough! here's the punishment.—*Forwaaaaaaaaaaaard, march!*

Agh! the lungs are on fire, the temples groan! The night rotates inside my eyes in this sunlight! The heart... the limbs. . . .

Où va-t-on? au combat? Je suis faible! les autres avancent. Les outils, les armes... le temps!...

Feu! feu sur moi! Là! ou je me rends.—Lâches!—Je me tue! Je me jette aux pieds des chevaux!

Ah!...

—Je m'y habituerai.

—Ce serait la vie française, le sentier de l'honneur!

Where are we heading? to battle? I feel weak! the others are moving ahead. Tools, weapons... time...!

Shoot! shoot me! Here! or I'll surrender.—Cowards!—I'll kill myself! I'll hurl myself under the horses!

Ah...!

—I'll get used to it.

—That would be the French way of life, the path of honor!

J'ai avalé une fameuse gorgée de poison.—Trois fois béni soit le con-
seil qui m'est arrivé!—Les entrailles me brûlent. La violence du venin
tord mes membres, me rend difforme, me terrasse. Je meurs de soif,
j'étouffe, je ne puis crier. C'est l'enfer, l'éternelle peine! Voyez comme
le feu se relève! Je brûle comme il faut. Va, démon!

J'avais entrevu la conversion au bien et au bonheur, le salut. Puis-je
décrire la vision, l'air de l'enfer ne souffre pas les hymnes! C'était des
millions de créatures charmantes, un suave concert spirituel, la force et
la paix, les nobles ambitions, que sais-je?

Les nobles ambitions!

Et c'est encore la vie!—Si la damnation est éternelle! Un homme qui
veut se mutiler est bien damné, n'est-ce pas? Je me crois en enfer, donc
j'y suis. C'est l'exécution du catéchisme. Je suis esclave de mon
baptême. Parents, vous avez fait mon malheur et vous avez fait le vôtre.
Pauvre innocent!—L'enfer ne peut attaquer les païens.—C'est la vie en-
core! Plus tard, les délices de la damnation seront plus profondes. Un
crime, vite, que je tombe au néant, de par la loi humaine.

Tais-toi, mais tais-toi!... C'est la honte, le reproche, ici: Satan qui
dit que le feu est ignoble, que ma colère est affreusement sotte.—
Assez!... Des erreurs qu'on me souffle, magies, parfums faux, musi-
ques puériles.—Et dire que je tiens la vérité, que je vois la justice: j'ai
un jugement sain et arrêté, je suis prêt pour la perfection... Orgueil.—
La peau de ma tête se dessèche. Pitié! Seigneur, j'ai peur. J'ai soif, si
soif! Ah! l'enfance, l'herbe, la pluie, le lac sur les pierres, *le clair de lune
quand le clocher sonnait douze*... le diable est au clocher, à cette heure.
Marie! Sainte-Vierge!... —Horreur de ma bêtise.

Là-bas, ne sont-ce pas des âmes honnêtes, qui me veulent du
bien... Venez... J'ai un oreiller sur la bouche, elles ne m'entendent
pas, ce sont des fantômes. Puis, jamais personne ne pense à autrui.
Qu'on n'approche pas. Je sens le roussi, c'est certain.

Les hallucinations sont innombrables. C'est bien ce que j'ai toujours
eu: plus de foi en l'histoire, l'oubli des principes. Je m'en tairai: poètes
et visionnaires seraient jaloux. Je suis mille fois le plus riche, soyons
avare comme la mer.

I've swallowed a terrific mouthful of poison.—Blessings three times over on the impulse that came to me!—My guts are on fire. The poison's violence twists my limbs, deforms me, knocks me down. I'm dying of thirst, I'm choking, I can't scream. It's hell, endless pain! Look how the fire flashes up! I'm burning nicely. Go on, demon!

I'd caught a glimpse of conversion to goodness and happiness, salvation. Can I describe the vision? Hell's atmosphere won't suffer hymns! There were millions of charming people, a sweet spiritual concert, strength and peace, noble ambitions, who knows?

Noble ambitions!

And this is still life!—What if damnation's everlasting! A man who wants to mutilate himself is pretty well damned, right? I think I'm in hell, therefore I am. It's the catechism come true. I'm the slave of my baptism. Parents, you've created my tortures and yours.—Poor nitwit! Hell can't wield power over pagans.—This is still life! Later on, the delights of damnation will be much deeper. A crime, quick, so I can plunge into nothingness in accordance with human law.

Shut up, will you shut up...! There's disgrace and reproaches here—Satan who says the fire's contemptible, who says my temper's desperately silly.—Enough...! Errors they're whispering to me, magic, misleading perfumes, childish music.—And to think I'm dealing in truth, I'm looking at justice: my reasoning powers are sane and sound, I'm ready for perfection... Pride.—My scalp is drying up. Help! Lord, I'm scared. I'm thirsty, so thirsty! O childhood, the grass, the rain, the lake water on stones, *the moonlight when the bell struck twelve*.... The devil's in the tower right now. Mary! Holy Virgin...!— Loathing for my blunder.

Out there, aren't those virtuous souls who are wishing me well...? Come.... I've got a pillow over my mouth, they won't hear me, they're ghosts. Besides, no one ever thinks of others. Don't come near me. I smell of heresy, that's for sure.

No end to these hallucinations. It's exactly what I've always known: no more faith in history, principles forgotten. I'll keep quiet: poets and visionaries would be jealous. I'm a thousand times richer, let's be miserly like the sea.

Ah çà! l'horloge de la vie s'est arrêtée tout à l'heure. Je ne suis plus au monde.—La théologie est sérieuse, l'enfer est certainement *en bas*— et le ciel en haut.—Extase, cauchemar, sommeil dans un nid de flammes.

Que de malices dans l'attention dans la campagne... Satan, Ferdinand, court avec les graines sauvages... Jésus marche sur les ronces purpurines, sans les courber... Jésus marchait sur les eaux irritées. La lanterne nous le montra debout, blanc et des tresses brunes, au flanc d'une vague d'émeraude...

Je vais dévoiler tous les mystères: mystères religieux ou naturels, mort, naissance, avenir, passé, cosmogonie, néant. Je suis maître en fantasmagories.

Écoutez!...

J'ai tous les talents!—Il n'y a personne ici et il y a quelqu'un: je ne voudrais pas répandre mon trésor.—Veut-on des chants nègres, des danses de houris?—Veut-on que je disparaisse, que je plonge à la recherche de l'*anneau?* Veut-on? Je ferai de l'or, des remèdes.

Fiez-vous donc à moi, la foi soulage, guide, guérit. Tous, venez,— même les petits enfants,—que je vous console, qu'on répande pour vous son coeur,—le coeur merveilleux!—Pauvres hommes, travailleurs! Je ne demande pas de prières; avec votre confiance seulement, je serai heureux.

—Et pensons à moi. Ceci me fait peu regretter le monde. J'ai de la chance de ne pas souffrir plus. Ma vie ne fut que folies douces, c'est regrettable.

Bah! faisons toutes les grimaces imaginables.

Décidément, nous sommes hors du monde. Plus aucun son. Mon tact a disparu. Ah! mon château, ma Saxe, mon bois de saules. Les soirs, les matins, les nuits, les jours... Suis-je las!

Je devrais avoir mon enfer pour la colère, mon enfer pour l'orgueil,—et l'enfer de la caresse; un concert d'enfers.

Je meurs de lassitude. C'est le tombeau, je m'en vais aux vers, horreur de l'horreur! Satan, farceur, tu veux me dissoudre, avec tes charmes. Je réclame. Je réclame! un coup de fourche, une goutte de feu.

Ah! remonter à la vie! Jeter les yeux sur nos difformités. Et ce poison, ce baiser mille fois maudit! Ma faiblesse, la cruauté du monde! Mon Dieu, pitié, cachez-moi, je me tiens trop mal!—Je suis caché et je ne le suis pas.

C'est le feu qui se relève avec son damné.

Well now! the clock of life stopped a few minutes ago. I'm not in the world any more.—Theology's a serious thing, hell is certainly *way down*—and heaven's above.—Ecstasy, nightmare, sleep in a nest of flames.

How malicious one's outlook in the country... Satan—Old Scratch —goes running around with the wild grain... Jesus is walking on the blackberry bushes without bending them... Jesus used to walk on troubled waters. The lantern revealed him to us, standing, pale with long brownish hair, on the crest of an emerald wave....

I'm going to unveil all the mysteries: religious mysteries or natural, death, birth, future, past, cosmogony, nothingness. I'm a master of hallucinations.

Listen...!

I've got all the talents!—There's no one here and there's someone: I wouldn't want to waste my treasure.—Do you want nigger songs, houri dances? Do you want me to disappear, to dive down for the *ring?* Do you want that? I'm going to make gold... remedies.

Then have faith in me, faith is soothing, it guides, it cures. Come, all of you—even the little children—and I'll comfort you, I'll spill out my heart for you,—the marvelous heart!—Poor men, workers! I don't ask for your prayers. With your trust alone, I'll be happy.

—And what about me? All of this doesn't make me miss the world much. I'm lucky not to suffer more. My life was nothing but lovely mistakes, it's too bad.

Bah! let's make every possible ugly face.

We're out of the world, for sure. Not even a sound. My touch has disappeared. Ah, my castle, my Saxony, my willow woods. Evenings, mornings, nights, days... I'm worn out!

I should have my hell for anger, my hell for conceit—and the hell of caresses: a concert of hells.

I'm dying of tiredness. It's the grave, horror of horrors, I'm going to the worms! Satan, you joker, you want to melt me down with your charms. I demand it, I demand it! a poke of the pitchfork, a drop of fire.

Ah, to come back to life again! To feast my eyes on our deformities. And that poison, that kiss a thousand times damned! My weakness, the world's cruelty! My God, mercy, hide me, I always misbehave!—I'm hidden and then again I'm not.

It's the fire flaring up again with its damned!

DÉLIRES I

VIERGE FOLLE / L'ÉPOUX INFERNAL

Écoutons la confession d'un compagnon d'enfer:

«Ô divin Époux, mon Seigneur, ne refusez pas la confession de la plus triste de vos servantes. Je suis perdue. Je suis soûle. Je suis impure. Quelle vie!

«Pardon, divin Seigneur, pardon! Ah! pardon! Que de larmes! Et que de larmes encore plus tard, j'espère!

«Plus tard, je connaîtrai le divin Époux! Je suis née soumise à Lui.— L'autre peut me battre maintenant!

«À présent, je suis au fond du monde! Ô mes amies!... non, pas mes amies... Jamais délires ni tortures semblables... Est-ce bête!

«Ah! je souffre, je crie. Je souffre vraiment. Tout pourtant m'est permis, chargée du mépris des plus méprisables coeurs.

«Enfin, faisons cette confidence, quitte à la répéter vingt autres fois,—aussi morne, aussi insignifiante!

«Je suis esclave de l'Époux infernal, celui qui a perdu les vierges folles. C'est bien ce démon-là. Ce n'est pas un spectre, ce n'est pas un fantôme. Mais moi qui ai perdu la sagesse, qui suis damnée et morte au monde,—on ne me tuera pas!—Comment vous le décrire! Je ne sais même plus parler. Je suis en deuil, je pleure, j'ai peur. Un peu de fraîcheur, Seigneur, si vous voulez, si vous voulez bien!

«Je suis veuve... —J'étais veuve... —mais oui, j'ai été bien sérieuse jadis, et je ne suis pas née pour devenir squelette!... Lui était presque un enfant... Ses délicatesses mystérieuses m'avaient séduite. J'ai oublié tout mon devoir humain pour le suivre. Quelle vie! La vraie vie est absente. Nous ne sommes pas au monde. Je vais où il va, il le faut. Et souvent il s'emporte contre moi, *moi, la pauvre âme*. Le Démon!—C'est un Démon, vous savez, *ce n'est pas un homme*.

«Il dit "Je n'aime pas les femmes. L'amour est à réinventer, on le sait. Elles ne peuvent plus que vouloir une position assurée. La position gagnée, coeur et beauté sont mis de côté: il ne reste que froid dédain, l'aliment du mariage, aujourd'hui. Ou bien je vois des femmes, avec les signes du bonheur, dont, moi, j'aurais pu faire de bonnes camarades, dévorées tout d'abord par des brutes sensibles comme des bûchers..."

DELIRIUM I

FOOLISH VIRGIN / HELLISH BRIDEGROOM

Let's listen to a hell-mate's confession:

"O heavenly Bridegroom, my Lord, please don't reject the confession of the saddest of your servant girls. I'm lost. I'm drunk. I'm impure. What a life!

"Forgive me, heavenly Lord, forgive me! Ah, forgive me! Lots of tears! And lots more tears later on, I hope!

"Later on, I'll get to know the heavenly Bridegroom! I was born to submit to Him.—The other one can beat me for the time being!

"Right now, I'm at the bottom of the world, O my friends!... no, not my friends.... Never such delirium and tortures as these.... How idiotic!

"Aaaaaaah, I'm suffering, I'm screaming. I'm really suffering. Still, everything's permitted me—burdened with the contempt of the most contemptible hearts.

"Anyway, let's make this admission, at the risk of repeating it another twenty times—as dreary, as insignificant as ever!

"I'm a slave of the hellish Bridegroom, the one who seduced the foolish virgins. That's the very devil he is. He's not a fantasy, he's not a ghost. But I, who've lost all control, who've become damned and dead to the world—they won't kill me!—How can I describe them? I can't even talk any more. I'm in mourning, I weep, I'm scared. A bit of fresh air, Lord, if you want—only if you want!

"I'm a widow... —I was a widow... —well yes, I used to be serious once, and I wasn't born to become a skeleton...! As for him, he was almost a child.... His mysterious delicacies had seduced me. I forgot all my human duties and followed him. What a life! Real life doesn't exist. We're not even born. I go where he goes, I've got to. And many times he gets screaming mad at me—*me, poor thing*. The devil!—He's a devil, you know, *he's not a man*.

"He says: 'I don't like women. Love's got to be reinvented, that's obvious. All they're able to grasp is the need for security. Once they've got it, feelings and beauty are put aside: all that's left is cool disdain, the food of marriage these days. Or else I see women with the earmarks of happiness, with whom I could've been close friends, swallowed up right away by brutes with the sensitivity of wood-sheds...'

«Je l'écoute faisant de l'infamie une gloire, de la cruauté un charme. "Je suis de race lointaine: mes pères étaient Scandinaves: ils se perçaient les côtes, buvaient leur sang.—Je me ferai des entailles partout le corps, je me tatouerai, je veux devenir hideux comme un Mongol: tu verras, je hurlerai dans les rues. Je veux devenir bien fou de rage. Ne me montre jamais de bijoux, je ramperais et me tordrais sur le tapis. Ma richesse, je la voudrais tachée de sang partout. Jamais je ne travaillerai... " Plusieurs nuits, son démon me saisissant, nous nous roulions, je luttais avec lui!—Les nuits, souvent, ivre, il se poste dans des rues ou dans des maisons, pour m'épouvanter mortellement.—"On me coupera vraiment le cou; ce sera dégoûtant." Oh! ces jours où il veut marcher avec l'air du crime!

«Parfois il parle, en une façon de patois attendri, de la mort qui fait repentir, des malheureux qui existent certainement, des travaux pénibles, des départs qui déchirent les coeurs. Dans les bouges où nous nous enivrions, il pleurait en considérant ceux qui nous entouraient, bétail de la misère. Il relevait les ivrognes dans les rues noires. Il avait la pitié d'une mère méchante pour les petits enfants.—Il s'en allait avec des gentillesses de petite fille au catéchisme.—Il feignait d'être éclairé sur tout, commerce, art, médecine.—Je le suivais, il le faut!

«Je voyais tout le décor dont, en esprit, il s'entourait; vêtements, draps, meubles: je lui prêtais des armes, une autre figure. Je voyais tout ce qui le touchait, comme il aurait voulu le créer pour lui. Quand il me semblait avoir l'esprit inerte, je le suivais, moi, dans des actions étranges et compliquées, loin, bonnes ou mauvaises: j'étais sûre de ne jamais entrer dans son monde. À côté de son cher corps endormi, que d'heures des nuits j'ai veillé, cherchant pourquoi il voulait tant s'évader de la réalité. Jamais homme n'eut pareil voeu. Je reconnaissais,—sans craindre pour lui,—qu'il pouvait être un sérieux danger dans la société.—Il a peut-être des secrets pour *changer la vie?* Non, il ne fait qu'en chercher, me répliquais-je. Enfin sa charité est ensorcelée, et j'en suis la prisonnière. Aucune autre âme n'aurait assez de force,—force de désespoir! pour la supporter,—pour être protégée et aimée par lui. D'ailleurs, je ne me le figurais pas avec une autre âme: on voit son Ange, jamais l'Ange d'un autre,—je crois. J'étais dans son âme comme dans un palais qu'on a vidé pour ne pas voir une personne si peu noble que vous: voilà tout. Hélas! je dépendais bien de lui. Mais que voulait-il avec mon existence terne et lâche? Il ne me rendait pas meilleure, s'il ne me faisait pas mourir! Tristement dépitée, je lui dis quelquefois: "Je te comprends." Il haussait les épaules.

"I listen to him turning disgrace into glory, cruelty into grace. 'I belong to a faraway race: my forbears were Scandinavians. They used to pierce their sides, drink their own blood.—I'm going to gash myself all over, tattoo my whole body, I want to be as hideous as a Mongol: you'll see, I'll be howling in the streets. I want to become insane with rage. Don't ever show me jewels, I'd crawl and writhe on the carpet. My wealth, I'd like it splattered with blood all over. I'll never work...' Many nights his devil would lay hold of me, we'd roll on the floor, I'd wrestle with him!—Many times at night, drunk, he hides there waiting for me in the streets, or behind houses, to scare the life out of me.—'They're really going to chop my head off. It'll be disgusting.' O those days when he wants to swagger with an air of crime!

"Sometimes he talks, in a kind of touching dialect, about death which can make you repent, about the miserable people who certainly exist, about irksome jobs, about separations that tear the heart. In the dives where we'd get drunk, he used to weep just looking at the people around us—down-and-out livestock. He'd pick up drunkards in dark streets. He had the pity of a rotten mother for little kids.—He walked around with the gentleness of a little girl going to catechism.—He made believe he knew everything there was to know about everything—business, art, medicine.—I followed him, I have to!

"I saw the whole decor he surrounded himself with in his own mind: clothes, sheets, furniture. I lent him weapons, another face. I looked at everything in relation to him, as he'd have liked to create it for himself. Whenever he'd look absent-minded, I'd follow him into weird and complicated strategies, far out, good or bad—I was sure I'd never get into his world. Next to his gorgeous sleeping body, how many hours I used to spend awake at night, wondering why he wanted to escape from reality so badly. No man ever had such a wish. I realized—without any fear for him—that he could be a serious threat to society.—Maybe he's got secrets *to change life?* No, he's only looking for some, I'd say to myself. His charity's bewitched, in short, and I'm its prisoner. No other soul would have the strength—the strength of despair!—to endure it, to be protected and loved by him. Besides, I couldn't imagine him with another soul: you see your Angel, never someone else's Angel—I think. I was in his soul as in a palace you've vacated so nobody plebean like yourself can be seen: that's it. Alas, I was really dependent on him! Yet what did he need my dull and spineless existence for? He wasn't making me any better—when he wasn't killing me outright! Out of sadness and spite, I'd sometimes tell him: 'I understand you.' He'd shrug his shoulders.

«Ainsi, mon chagrin se renouvelant sans cesse, et me trouvant plus égarée à mes yeux,—comme à tous les yeux qui auraient voulu me fixer, si je n'eusse été condamnée pour jamais à l'oubli de tous!—j'avais de plus en plus faim de sa bonté. Avec ses baisers et ses étreintes amies, c'était bien un ciel, un sombre ciel, où j'entrais, et où j'aurais voulu être laissée, pauvre, sourde, muette, aveugle. Déjà j'en prenais l'habitude. Je nous voyais comme deux bons enfants, libres de se promener dans le Paradis de tristesse. Nous nous accordions. Bien émus, nous travaillions ensemble. Mais, après une pénétrante caresse, il disait: "Comme ça te paraîtra drôle, quand je n'y serai plus, ce par quoi tu as passé. Quand tu n'auras plus mes bras sous ton cou, ni mon coeur pour t'y reposer, ni cette bouche sur tes yeux. Parce qu'il faudra que je m'en aille, très loin, un jour. Puis il faut que j'en aide d'autres: c'est mon devoir. Quoique ce ne soit guère ragoûtant..., chère âme... " Tout de suite je me pressentais, lui parti, en proie au vertige, précipitée dans l'ombre la plus affreuse: la mort. Je lui faisais promettre qu'il ne me lâcherait pas. Il l'a faite vingt fois, cette promesse d'amant. C'était aussi frivole que moi lui disant: "Je te comprends."

«Ah! je n'ai jamais été jalouse de lui. Il ne me quittera pas, je crois. Que devenir? Il n'a pas une connaissance, il ne travaillera jamais. Il veut vivre somnambule. Seules, sa bonté et sa charité lui donneraient-elles droit dans le monde réel? Par instants, j'oublie la pitié où je suis tombée: lui me rendra forte, nous voyagerons, nous chasserons dans les déserts, nous dormirons sur les pavés des villes inconnues, sans soins, sans peines. Ou je me réveillerai, et les lois et les moeurs auront changé,—grâce à son pouvoir magique,—le monde, en restant le même, me laissera à mes désirs, joies, nonchalances. Oh! la vie d'aventures qui existe dans les livres des enfants, pour me récompenser, j'ai tant souffert, me la donneras-tu? Il ne peut pas. J'ignore son idéal. Il m'a dit avoir des regrets, des espoirs: cela ne doit pas me regarder. Parle-t-il à Dieu? Peut-être devrais-je m'adresser à Dieu. Je suis au plus profond de l'abîme, et je ne sais plus prier.

«S'il m'expliquait ses tristesses, les comprendrais-je plus que ses railleries? Il m'attaque, il passe des heures à me faire honte de tout ce qui m'a pu toucher au monde, et s'indigne si je pleure.

"So, since my grief was always being renewed and since I looked more hopeless than ever in my own eyes—as in the eyes of everyone who would've observed me if I hadn't been condemned to oblivion forever by everyone!—I kept hungering more and more for his goodness. With his kisses and his loving hugs, it was really heaven—a dark heaven—which I entered and which I'd have liked to become stranded in, poor, deaf, dumb, blind. I'd now become completely hooked. I saw us as two good children, free to walk around in the Paradise of sadness. We got along fine. Deeply moved, we worked together. But after a penetrating caress, he'd say: 'How queer it'll all seem, when I'm no longer here, what you've gone through. When you don't have my arms around your neck any more, or my heart to lie down on, or this mouth on your eyes. Because some day I'll have to go, very far. And I must help others: it's my duty. Even though it's not terribly appetizing... dear heart. . . . ' Right away I could see myself, with him gone, in the clutch of vertigo, plunging down into deepest darkness: death. I'd make him promise never to ditch me. He made it twenty times, that lovers' promise. It was as flip as when I used to tell him: 'I understand you.'

"Look, I've never been jealous of him. He'll never leave me, I keep thinking. What would he do? He doesn't know a thing. He'll never work. He wants to live a sleepwalker's life. Do his goodness and charity alone give him the right to live in the real world? At times, I forget the depths I've fallen to: he'll make me strong, we'll go traveling, we'll hunt in deserted places, we'll sleep on the sidewalks of unknown cities, with no worries or griefs. Or else I'll wake up, and the laws and customs will've changed—thanks to his magic powers—or the world, while staying the same, will leave me my desires and joys and carefree ways. Oh! the life of adventure that's found in children's books, will you give it to me to reward me for all the things I've suffered? He can't do it. I don't know what his aims are. He told me he's got regrets, hopes: that's none of my business. Does he talk to God? Maybe I should ask God. I'm in the lower depths of the abyss and I don't know how to pray any more.

"If he explained his sorrows to me, would I understand them better than his mockeries? He attacks me, he spends hours making me feel ashamed of everything that ever touched me in this world, and gets furious if I cry.

«"Tu vois cet élégant jeune homme, entrant dans la belle et calme maison: il s'appelle Duval, Dufour, Armand, Maurice, que sais-je? Une femme s'est dévouée à aimer ce méchant idiot: elle est morte, c'est certes une sainte au ciel, à présent. Tu me feras mourir comme il a fait mourir cette femme. C'est notre sort, à nous, coeurs charitables... " Hélas! il avait des jours où tous les hommes agissant lui paraissaient les jouets de délires grotesques: il riait affreusement, longtemps.—Puis, il reprenait ses manières de jeune mère, de soeur aimée. S'il était moins sauvage, nous serions sauvés! Mais sa douceur aussi est mortelle. Je lui suis soumise.—Ah! je suis folle!

«Un jour peut-être il disparaîtra merveilleusement; mais il faut que je sache, s'il doit remonter à un ciel, que je voie un peu l'assomption de mon petit ami!»

Drôle de ménage!

" 'Do you see that elegant young man going into the nice refined house: his name's Duval, Dufours, Armand, Maurice, how should I know? A woman devoted her whole life to loving that filthy jackass: she's dead, she's a saint in heaven now for sure. You'll kill me the way he killed that woman. That's what happens to loving hearts like us. . . .'
Ah, there were days when all active men seemed to him grotesquely ridiculous playthings. He'd laugh horribly, on and on.—Then, he'd switch right back to the manners of a young mother or a big sister. If he were less wild, we'd be saved! But his sweetness too is deadly. I'm his slave. Ah! I'm insane!

"One day maybe he'll disappear in some miraculous way. But I've simply got to discover if he's due to go up to heaven so I'll be sure to catch a glimpse of the ascension of my luscious little lover!"

A queer twosome!

ALCHIMIE DU VERBE

À moi. L'histoire d'une de mes folies.

Depuis longtemps je me vantais de posséder tous les paysages possibles, et trouvais dérisoires les célébrités de la peinture et de la poésie moderne.

J'aimais les peintures idiotes, dessus de portes, décors, toiles de saltimbanques, enseignes, enluminures populaires; la littérature démodée, latin d'église, livres érotiques sans orthographe, romans de nos aïeules, contes de fées, petits livres de l'enfance, opéras vieux, refrains niais, rhythmes naïfs.

Je rêvais croisades, voyages de découvertes dont on n'a pas de relations, républiques sans histoires, guerres de religion étouffées, révolutions de moeurs, déplacements de races et de continents: je croyais à tous les enchantements.

J'inventai la couleur des voyelles!—*A* noir, *E* blanc, *I* rouge, *O* bleu, *U* vert.—Je réglai la forme et le mouvement de chaque consonne, et, avec des rhythmes instinctifs, je me flattai d'inventer un verbe poétique accessible, un jour ou l'autre, à tous les sens. Je réservais la traduction.

Ce fut d'abord une étude. J'écrivais des silences, des nuits, je notais l'inexprimable. Je fixais des vertiges.

————————

Loin des oiseaux, des troupeaux, des villageoises,
Que buvais-je, à genoux dans cette bruyère

Entourée de tendres bois de noisetiers,
Dans un brouillard d'après-midi tiède et vert?

Que pouvais-je boire dans cette jeune Oise,
—Ormeaux sans voix, gazon sans fleurs, ciel couvert!—

Boire à ces gourdes jaunes, loin de ma case
Chérie? Quelque liqueur d'or qui fait suer.

DELIRIUM II

ALCHEMY OF THE WORD

Now me. The story of one of my imbecilities.

For a long time I'd boasted of knowing all possible landscapes inside-out and liked to poke fun at the celebrities of modern painting and poetry.

I loved idiotic paintings, door panelings, stage sets, backdrops for acrobats, street signs, popular prints, old-fashioned literature, church Latin, erotic books with terrible spelling, the novels of our grandmothers, fairy tales, little childhood storybooks, old operas, nincompoop refrains, naive rhythms.

I dreamed up crusades, voyages of discovery that haven't been recorded yet, republics with no history, hushed-up religious wars, revolutions in folk customs, displacements of nations and continents: I believed in all kinds of wizardry.

I invented the colors of the vowels!—*A* black, *E* white, *I* red, *O* blue, *U* green.—I regulated the form and movement of every consonant and, with instinctive rhythms, I prided myself on inventing a poetic language accessible to all the senses sooner or later. I reserved translation rights.

In the beginning it was trial and error. I was writing silences, writing nights. I scribbled the inexpressible. I pinned down vertigos!

———————

Far from birds, from herds, from home-town girls,
What was I drinking on my knees in the bushes

With hazelnut trees all around me
In the lukewarm green of an afternoon mist?

What could I drink in that young Oise
—Trees with no voices, grass with no flowers, sky with no sun!

To drink from those yellow gourds, far from the cabin
I like? Liquors of gold that make you sweat.

Je faisais une louche enseigne d'auberge.
—Un orage vint chasser le ciel. Au soir
L'eau des bois se perdait sur les sables vierges,
Le vent de Dieu jetait des glaçons aux mares;

Pleurant, je voyais de l'or—et ne pus boire.—

———————

À quatre heures du matin, l'été,
Le sommeil d'amour dure encore.
Sous les bocages s'évapore
　　L'odeur du soir fêté.

Là-bas, dans leur vaste chantier
Au soleil des Hespérides,
Déjà s'agitent—en bras de chemise—
　　Les Charpentiers.

Dans leurs Déserts de mousse, tranquilles,
Ils préparent les lambris précieux
　　Où la ville
　　Peindra de faux cieux.

Ô, pour ces Ouvriers charmants
Sujets d'un roi de Babylone,
Vénus! quitte un instant les Amants
　　Dont l'âme est en couronne.

　　Ô Reine des Bergers,
Porte aux travailleurs l'eau-de-vie,
Que leurs forces soient en paix
En attendant le bain dans la mer à midi.

———————

La vieillerie poétique avait une bonne part dans mon alchimie du verbe.

I made a pretty poor sign for a tavern.
—A storm was hassling the sky. At night
The wet of the woods ran out on virgin sands,
God's wind tossed icicles in the ponds:

Weeping, I saw gold—and couldn't drink.—

————————

At four in the morning, summers,
The sexual sleep still lasts.
Under the trees, the love-feast's smells
    Evaporate.

Out there, in their huge lumberyards,
Under occidental sunlight,
Already busy as bees—in shirtsleeves—
    The Shipwrights.

In their Deserts of Foam, quietly,
They're preparing fabulous ceilings
    Where the city
Will paint fraudulent skies.

For the sake of these workingmen,
Subjects of a Babylonian king—
Venus! leave for a while the Lovers
    Whose souls are crowned!

    O Queen of Herds,
Bring the workers a little brandy
So their strength will feel no hurt
While they wait for their swim in the sea.

————————

Out-dated poetic tricks played a big part in my alchemy of the word.

Je m'habituai à l'hallucination simple: je voyais très-franchement une mosquée à la place d'une usine, une école de tambours faite par des anges, des calèches sur les routes du ciel, un salon au fond d'un lac; les monstres, les mystères; un titre de vaudeville dressait des épouvantes devant moi.

Puis j'expliquai mes sophismes magiques avec l'hallucination des mots!

Je finis par trouver sacré le désordre de mon esprit. J'étais oisif, en proie à une lourde fièvre: j'enviais la félicité des bêtes,—les chenilles, qui représentent l'innocence des limbes, les taupes, le sommeil de la virginité!

Mon caractère s'aigrissait. Je disais adieu au monde dans d'espèces de romances:

CHANSON DE LA PLUS HAUTE TOUR

Qu'il vienne, qu'il vienne,
Le temps dont on s'éprenne.

J'ai tant fait patience
Qu'à jamais j'oublie.
Craintes et souffrances
Aux cieux sont parties.
Et la soif malsaine
Obscurcit mes veines.

Qu'il vienne, qu'il vienne,
Le temps dont on s'éprenne.

Telle la prairie
À l'oubli livrée,
Grandie, et fleurie
D'encens et d'ivraies,
Au bourdon farouche
Des sales mouches.

I got used to elementary hallucination. I could very precisely see a mosque where there was a mere factory, a corps of drummer-boys made up of angels, ponycoaches on the highways of heavens, a living-room at the bottom of a lake—monsters, mysteries—the title of a vaudeville show set up real horrors before me.

Then I'd justify my magic sophistries with the hallucination of words!

I ended up viewing the disorder of my mind as sacred. I was passive, the victim of a heavy feverishness: I envied the happiness of animals—the caterpillars that represent the innocence of limbo—the moles, the sleep of virginity!

My temper was turning sour. I said farewell to the world in this sort of light-hearted love-song:

SONG OF THE TALLEST TOWER

Let it come, let it come,
The time we've all been dreaming of.

I've waited such a long while
I've lost track of my past.
All fears and all guile
Have gone to heaven at last.
And an unwholesome thirst
Proves my blood is cursed.

Let it come, let it come,
The time we've all been dreaming of.

Like the green fields
Fallen to oblivion,
Flowering, overgrown
With incense and weeds,
It hums its grim lies
Like filthy flies.

Qu'il vienne, qu'il vienne,
Le temps dont on s'éprenne.

———————

J'aimai le désert, les vergers brûlés, les boutiques fanées, les boissons
tiédies. Je me traînais dans les ruelles puantes et, les yeux fermés, je
m'offrais au soleil, dieu de feu.

«Général, s'il reste un vieux canon sur tes remparts en ruines,
bombarde-nous avec des blocs de terre sèche. Aux glaces des magasins
splendides! dans les salons! Fais manger sa poussière à la ville. Oxyde
les gargouilles. Emplis les boudoirs de poudre de rubis brûlantes...»

Oh! le moucheron enivré à la pissotière de l'auberge, amoureux de la
bourrache, et que dissout un rayon!

FAIM

Si j'ai du goût, ce n'est guère
Que pour la terre et les pierres.
Je déjeune toujours d'air,
De roc, de charbons, de fer.

Mes faims, tournez. Paissez, faims
        Le pré des sons.
Attirez le gai venin
        Des liserons.

Mangez les cailloux qu'on brise,
Les vieilles pierres d'églises;
Les galets des vieux déluges,
Pains semés dans les vallées grises.

———————

Le loup criait sous les feuilles
En crachant les belles plumes
De son repas de volailles:
Comme lui je me consume.

Let it come, let it come,
The time we've all been dreaming of.

———————

I loved the desert, burnt up orchards, musty shops, tepid drinks. I hung around the stinking alleys and, with eyes closed, I offered myself to the sun, god of fire.

"General, if there's an old cannon left on your demolished ramparts, fire away with lumps of dried-up muck. At the mirrors in magnificent stores! at the living-rooms! Make the city eat its own dust. Oxidize the gargoyles. Fill the bedrooms with the red-hot powder of rubies. . . . "

O the tipsy little fly in the tavern piss-pot, in love with diuretic smells, liquidated by a sunbeam!

HUNGER

If I've got taste, it's not
Strictly for dirt and stones.
My breakfast's always air,
Rocks, charcoal, steel.

My hungers, *turn!* Hungers,
Nibble on a field of sounds.
Suck in the gorgeous poisons
Of the prickly plants.

Eat up the crushed pebbles,
Old stones from churches,
Gravel from archaic floods,
Bread scattered in gray ditches.

———————

The wolf howled under the leaves
While spitting fine feathers out
From his feast of fowl:
Like him, I devour myself.

Les salades, les fruits
N'attendent que la cueillette;
Mais l'araignée de la haie
Ne mange que des violettes.

Que je dorme! que je bouille
Aux autels de Salomon.
Le bouillon court sur la rouille,
Et se mêle au Cédron.

Enfin, ô bonheur, ô raison, j'écartai du ciel l'azur, qui est du noir, et je vécus, étincelle d'or de la lumière *nature*. De joie, je prenais une expression bouffonne et égarée au possible:

Elle est retrouvée!
Quoi? l'éternité.
C'est la mer mêlée
    Au soleil.

Mon âme éternelle,
Observe ton voeu
Malgré la nuit seule
Et le jour en feu.

Donc tu te dégages
Des humains suffrages,
Des communs élans!
Tu voles selon...

—Jamais l'espérance.
    Pas d'*orietur*.
Science et patience,
Le supplice est sûr.

Plus de lendemain,
Braises de satin,
    Votre ardeur
    Est le devoir.

Lettuces and fruits
Are waiting there for the picking.
But the spider on the fence
Eats only violets.

Let me sleep! let me boil
At the altars of Solomon.
The broth drips down the mildew
And blends with the Kedron.

At last—O happiness, O reason—I wiped the blue which is black-
ness out of the sky, and I lived—a golden spark of *pure* light. Out of
sheer bliss, I put on an air as oafish and unhinged as possible:

It's found again!
—What?—*Eternity.*
It's the sun merging
With the sea.

My eternal soul,
Stick to your desire—
Despite the nights alone
And the day on fire.

This way you'll be free
From human idiocy,
From humdrum longing!
You fly according. . . .

—Not a trace of hope,
Never any *praying.*
Knowingness and patience,
Pain's a sure thing.

No more tomorrows,
Velvety ashes.
Your eagerness
Is the task.

Elle est retrouvée!
—Quoi?—l'Éternité.
C'est la mer mêlée
Au soleil.

———————

Je devins un opéra fabuleux: je vis que tous les êtres ont une fatalité de bonheur: l'action n'est pas la vie, mais une façon de gâcher quelque force, un énervement. La morale est la faiblesse de la cervelle.

À chaque être, plusieurs *autres* vies me semblaient dues. Ce monsieur ne sait ce qu'il fait: il est un ange. Cette famille est une nichée de chiens. Devant plusieurs hommes, je causai tout haut avec un moment d'une de leurs autres vies.—Ainsi, j'ai aimé un porc.

Aucun des sophismes de la folie,—la folie qu'on enferme,—n'a été oublié par moi: je pourrais les redire tous, je tiens le système.

Ma santé fut menacée. La terreur venait. Je tombais dans des sommeils de plusieurs jours, et, levé, je continuais les rêves les plus tristes. J'étais mûr pour le trépas, et par une route de dangers ma faiblesse me menait aux confins du monde et de la Cimmérie, patrie de l'ombre et des tourbillons.

Je dus voyager, distraire les enchantements assemblés sur mon cerveau. Sur la mer, que j'aimais comme si elle eût dû me laver d'une souillure, je voyais se lever la croix consolatrice. J'avais été damné par l'arc-en-ciel. Le Bonheur était ma fatalité, mon remords, mon ver: ma vie serait toujours trop immense pour être dévouée à la force et à la beauté.

Le Bonheur! Sa dent, douce à la mort, m'avertissait au chant du coq,—*ad matutinum,* au *Christus venit,*—dans les plus sombres villes:

Ô saisons, ô châteaux!
Quelle âme est sans défauts?

J'ai fait la magique étude
Du bonheur, qu'aucun n'élude.

Salut à lui, chaque fois
Que chante le coq gaulois.

It's found again!
—What?—Eternity.
It's the sun merging
    With the sea.

I became a fabulous opera. I saw that everybody's born with a fatal need for happiness: action isn't life, but a way of maiming some power, a mere irritant. Morality's the blind spot of the brain.

Everybody seemed to me to deserve lots of *other* lives. This gentleman doesn't know what he's doing: he's an angel. This family's a litter of puppies. With lots of people, I talked aloud with a split second from one of their lives.—That's how I came to love a pig.

I never forgot any of the trickeries of madness—madness fit to be locked up: I could repeat them all, I'm holding on to the key.

My sanity was threatened. Terror was near. I'd fall into deep sleep for days and when I got up, I'd go on dreaming the gloomiest dreams. I was ripe for death—and on a road brimming with risks, my weakness drove me to the outer limits of the world and of Kimmeria: land of shadows and whirlwinds.

I needed to travel, to sidetrack the witchcraft that crowded my brain. Over the ocean, which I loved as if it'd been about to cleanse me of filth, I saw the cross of consolation rising up. I'd been damned by the rainbow. Happiness was my fatal need, my remorse, my worm: my life would always be too immense to be devoted to strength and beauty.

Happiness! Its tooth, sweet enough to kill, warned me at the crowing of the cock—*ad matutinum,* at the *Christus venit*—in the darkest of cities:

O seasons, O castles!
What soul's without hassles!

Happiness was my pursuit,
And I've touched its root.

Here's to it: Greetings!
Each time the French cock sings.

Ah! je n'aurai plus d'envie:
Il s'est chargé de ma vie.

Ce charme a pris âme et corps
Et dispersé les efforts.

Ô saisons, ô châteaux!

L'heure de sa fuite, hélas!
Sera l'heure du trépas.

Ô saisons, ô châteaux!

———————

Cela s'est passé. Je sais aujourd'hui saluer la beauté.

No need to go on craving:
He knows which way I'm aiming.

This charm clinched body and soul
And made a flawless whole.

O seasons, O castles!

The time of its ultimate flight
Will be the hour of blight!

O seasons, O castles!

———————

That's over now. These days I know how to greet beauty.

Ah! cette vie de mon enfance, la grande route par tous les temps, sobre surnaturellement, plus désintéressé que le meilleur des mendiants, fier de n'avoir ni pays, ni amis, quelle sottise c'était. Et je m'en aperçois seulement!

—J'ai eu raison de mépriser ces bonshommes qui ne perdraient pas l'occasion d'une caresse, parasites de la propreté et de la santé de nos femmes, aujourd'hui qu'elles sont si peu d'accord avec nous.

J'ai eu raison dans tous mes dédains: puisque je m'évade!

Je m'évade!

Je m'explique.

Hier encore, je soupirais: «Ciel! sommes-nous assez de damnés icibas! Moi j'ai tant de temps déjà dans leur troupe! Je les connais tous. Nous nous reconnaissons toujours; nous nous dégoûtons. La charité nous est inconnue. Mais nous sommes polis; nos relations avec le monde sont très-convenables.» Est-ce étonnant? Le monde! les marchands, les naïfs!—Nous ne sommes pas déshonorés.—Mais les élus, comment nous recevraient-ils? Or il y a des gens hargneux et joyeux, de faux élus, puisqu'il nous faut de l'audace ou de l'humilité pour les aborder. Ce sont les seuls élus. Ce ne sont pas des bénisseurs!

M'étant retrouvé deux sous de raison—ça passe vite!—je vois que mes malaises viennent de ne m'être pas figuré assez tôt que nous sommes à l'Occident. Les marais occidentaux! Non que je croie la lumière altérée, la forme exténuée, le mouvement égaré... Bon! voici que mon esprit veut absolument se charger de tous les développements cruels qu'a subis l'esprit depuis la fin de l'Orient... Il en veut, mon esprit!

... Mes deux sous de raison sont finis!—L'esprit est autorité, il veut que je sois en Occident. Il faudrait le faire taire pour conclure comme je voulais.

J'envoyais au diable les palmes des martyrs, les rayons de l'art, l'orgueil des inventeurs, l'ardeur des pillards; je retournais a l'Orient et à la sagesse première et éternelle.—Il paraît que c'est un rêve de paresse grossière!

Ah, that childhood life of mine, the open road in and out of season, supernaturally sober, not giving a damn any more than the best of beggars, proud to have no country, no friends: what stupidity that was!—And I've just begun to realize it!

—I was right to despise those gay blades who'd never pass up a little ass-grabbing, parasites of the cleanness and healthiness of "our women," now that women seldom see eye-to-eye with us.

I was right in all my disdains—because I'm escaping!

I'm escaping!

Let me explain.

Even yesterday, I was sighing: "Good grief! aren't there enough of us damned ones down here! I know them all. We always recognize each other; we disgust each other. Charity's unknown among us. But we're polite; our relations with people are quite correct." Is this astonishing? People! businessmen, nitwits!—We're not disgraced.—But the elect, how would they receive us? Look, these are types who are bad-tempered and blissful, the phoney elect, since you've got to have guts or humility to approach them. They're the only elect. They're no sprinklers of holy water!

Since I've picked up two cents' worth of smarts—that's soon spent!—I can see that my anxieties come from not having figured out soon enough that we're in the Western World. The Western swamps! Not that I think the light diminished, the forms anemic, the momentum slowed down. . . . Well! look how my spirit insists on taking the blame for all the brutal developments which the Spirit's suffered since the eclipse of the East. . . . It's really willing, my spirit!

. . . My two cents' worth of reason's spent!—The spirit's in charge, it wants me to be in the Western World. I'd have to silence it to end up with my own conclusions.

I said *to hell* with the glories of martyrs, the sparkle of art, the pride of inventors, the eagerness of exploiters. I was going back to the East and to the first and everlasting wisdom.—It seems it's a dream of crass laziness.

Pourtant, je ne songeais guère au plaisir d'échapper aux souffrances modernes. Je n'avais pas en vue la sagesse bâtarde du Coran.—Mais n'y a-t-il pas un supplice réel en ce que, depuis cette déclaration de la science, le christianisme, l'homme *se joue,* se prouve les évidences, se gonfle du plaisir de répéter ces preuves, et ne vit que comme cela! Torture subtile, niaise; source de mes divagations spirituelles. La nature pourrait s'ennuyer, peut-être! M. Prudhomme est né avec le Christ.

N'est-ce pas parce que nous cultivons la brume! Nous mangeons la fièvre avec nos légumes aqueux. Et l'ivrognerie! et le tabac! et l'ignorance! et les dévouements!—Tout cela est-il assez loin de la pensée de la sagesse de l'Orient, la patrie primitive? Pourquoi un monde moderne, si de pareils poisons s'inventent!

Les gens d'Église diront: C'est compris. Mais vous voulez parler de l'Éden. Rien pour vous dans l'histoire des peuples orientaux.—C'est vrai; c'est à l'Éden que je songeais! Qu'est-ce que c'est pour mon rêve, cette pureté des races antiques!

Les philosophes: Le monde n'a pas d'âge. L'humanité se déplace, simplement. Vous êtes en Occident, mais libre d'habiter dans votre Orient, quelque ancien qu'il vous le faille,—et d'y habiter bien. Ne soyez pas un vaincu. Philosophes, vous êtes de votre Occident.

Mon esprit, prends garde. Pas de partis de salut violents. Exerce-toi!—Ah! la science ne va pas assez vite pour nous!

—Mais je m'aperçois que mon esprit dort.

S'il était bien éveillé toujours à partir de ce moment nous serions bientôt à la vérité, qui peut-être nous entoure avec ses anges pleurant!... —S'il avait été éveillé jusqu'à ce moment-ci, c'est que je n'aurais pas cédé aux instincts délétères, à une époque immémoriale!... —S'il avait toujours été bien éveillé, je voguerais en pleine sagesse!...

Ô pureté! pureté!

C'est cette minute d'éveil qui m'a donné la vision de la pureté!—Par l'esprit on va à Dieu!

Déchirante infortune!

Still, I hardly dreamed of the pleasure of escaping modern suffering. I didn't have the bastard wisdom of the Koran in mind.—But isn't there genuine torture in the fact that, ever since that manifesto of science, Christianity, man's been *kidding himself,* convincing himself of the obvious, inflating himself with the thrill of repeating the proofs, and just can't live any other way? Finicky torture, stupid—the root of my own psychic meanderings. Nature might get bored, perhaps! Mr.Play-It-Safe was born the same day as Christ.

Isn't it because we're cultivating fog? We eat fever with our watery vegetables. And drunkenness! and tobacco! and ignorance! and self-sacrifice!—And all that's a long shot from the wit and wisdom of the East, the primeval fatherland, isn't it? What good's a modern world if poisons like that are invented?

The clergyman will say: We see your point. But you're talking about Eden. Not a thing in the history of Western civilization for you.—That's true. It's Eden I was thinking of! What's that got to do with my dream, that purity of ancient races!

The philosophers: The world is ageless. The human race, quite simply, moves along. You're in the Western World, but you're free to live in your East, as ancient as you care to be—and quite comfortably. Never say die. Philosophers, you're stuck with your West.

O my soul, watch out. No violent schemes of salvation. Get busy!—Ah, science doesn't move fast enough for us!

—But I notice my soul's asleep.

If it kept staying wide awake from now on, we'd soon reach the truth which may be surrounding us with its weeping angels... ! If it'd been awake up to this point, I wouldn't have given in to my devastating instincts at a moment I'll never forget... ! If it'd always been awake, I'd be flying high on the breezes of wisdom... !

O purity! purity!

It's this moment of awakening that's given me the vision of purity!—Through spirit we hasten to God!

Shattering piece of luck!

Le travail humain! c'est l'explosion qui éclaire mon abîme de temps en temps.

«Rien n'est vanité; à la science, et en avant!» crie l'Ecclésiaste moderne, c'est-à-dire *Tout le monde*. Et pourtant les cadavres des méchants et des fainéants tombent sur le coeur des autres... Ah! vite, vite un peu; là-bas, par delà la nuit, ces récompenses futures, éternelles... les échappons-nous?...

—Qu'y puis-je? Je connais le travail; et la science est trop lente. Que la prière galope et que la lumière gronde... je le vois bien. C'est trop simple, et il fait trop chaud; on se passera de moi. J'ai mon devoir, j'en serai fier à la façon de plusieurs, en le mettant de côté.

Ma vie est usée. Allons! feignons, fainéantons, ô pitié! Et nous existerons en nous amusant, en rêvant amours monstres et univers fantastiques, en nous plaignant et en querellant les apparences du monde, saltimbanque, mendiant, artiste, bandit,—prêtre! Sur mon lit d'hôpital, l'odeur de l'encens m'est revenue si puissante; gardien des aromates sacrés, confesseur, martyr...

Je reconnais là ma sale éducation d'enfance. Puis quoi!... Aller mes vingt ans, si les autres vont vingt ans...

Non! non! à présent je me révolte contre la mort! Le travail paraît trop léger à mon orgueil: ma trahison au monde serait un supplice trop court. Au dernier moment, j'attaquerais à droite, à gauche...

Alors,—oh!—chère pauvre âme, l'éternité serait-elle pas perdue pour nous!

The work of the human race! that's the explosion that lights up my lower depths from time to time.

"Nothing's vanity. Move ahead with science!" shouts the modern Ecclesiastes, which is to say *everybody*. And yet the corpses of the wicked and the lazy plop down on the hearts of others. . . Ah! hurry, hurry a bit! Out there, beyond the night, those future rewards, everlasting. . . are we missing out on them?

—What can I do? I know what work is. And science is too slow. Prayer gallops along and the light rumbles. . . I see that too. It's too simple, and it's too hot. They'll do without me. I've got my job. I'll take pride in it the way others do—by laying it aside.

My life's used up. Come on! let's shirk, let's gold-brick, for pity's sake! And we'll go on enjoying ourselves, dreaming up monstrous loves and fantastic universes, griping and criticizing the world's disguises—acrobat, beggar, artist, outlaw—priest! On my hospital bed, the smell of incense came back to me, so potent: custodian of sacred aromatics, confessor, martyr. . . .

I recognize in that the filthy education of my childhood. So what. . .! Here's my twenty years, since others put in twenty years. . . .

No! no! I revolt right now against death! Work looks too lightweight to my pride: being betrayed to the world would be too brief a torture. At the last minute, I'd attack right and left. . . .

Then—oh!—poor dear soul, wouldn't eternity be lost for us!

N'eus-je pas *une fois* une jeunesse aimable, héroïque, fabuleuse, à écrire sur des feuilles d'or,—trop de chance! Par quel crime, par quelle erreur, ai-je mérité ma faiblesse actuelle? Vous qui prétendez que des bêtes poussent des sanglots de chagrin, que des malades désespèrent, que des morts rêvent mal, tâchez de raconter ma chute et mon sommeil. Moi, je ne puis pas plus m'expliquer que le mendiant avec ses continuels *Pater* et *Ave Maria. Je ne sais plus parler!*

Pourtant, aujourd'hui, je crois avoir fini la relation de mon enfer. C'était bien l'enfer; l'ancien, celui dont le fils de l'homme ouvrit les portes.

Du même désert, à la même nuit, toujours mes yeux las se réveillent à l'étoile d'argent, toujours, sans que s'émeuvent les rois de la vie, les trois mages, le coeur, l'âme, l'esprit. Quant irons-nous, par delà les grèves et les monts, saluer la naissance du travail nouveau, la sagesse nouvelle, la fuite des tyrans et des démons, la fin de la superstition, adorer—les premiers!—Noël sur la terre!

Le chant des cieux, la marche des peuples! Esclaves, ne maudissons pas la vie.

Didn't I *at one time* have a lovely boyhood—heroic, fabulous, worth writing about on golden sheets—worse luck! Through what crime, through what mistake did I deserve my current weakness? Those of you who pretend that animals sob with grief, that sick people despair, that the dead have bad dreams, *please* try to explain my fall and my sleep. As for me, I can no more make you see my point than the beggar with his endless Our Father's and Hail Mary's. *I don't know how to talk any more!*

Yet, today, I think I'm all through talking about my hell. It was really hell. The old hell, the one whose doors were thrown open by the Son of Man.

From the same desert, towards the same night, my tired eyes always wake up to the silver star, always, without ever managing to move the Kings of life, the three magi—the heart, the soul, the mind. When are we going to take off, past the shores and the mountains, to greet the new task, the new wisdom, the defeat of tyrants and devils, the end of superstition—to worship—the first to do so!—Christmas on this earth!

The music of the spheres, the march of peoples! Slaves, let's not curse this life.

ADIEU

L'automne déjà!—Mais pourquoi regretter un éternel soleil, si nous sommes engagés à la découverte de la clarté divine,—loin des gens qui meurent sur les saisons.

L'automne. Notre barque élevée dans les brumes immobiles tourne vers le port de la misère, la cité énorme au ciel taché de feu et de boue. Ah! les haillons pourris, le pain trempé de pluie, l'ivresse, les mille amours qui m'ont crucifié! Elle ne finira donc point cette goule reine de millions d'âmes et de corps morts *et qui seront jugés!* Je me revois la peau rongée par la boue et la peste des vers plein les cheveux et les aisselles et encore de plus gros vers dans le coeur, étendu parmi les inconnus sans âge, sans sentiment... J'aurais pu y mourir... L'affreuse évocation! J'exécute la misère.

Et je redoute l'hiver parce que c'est la saison du comfort!

—Quelquefois je vois au ciel des plages sans fin couvertes de blanches nations en joie. Un grand vaisseau d'or, au-dessus de moi, agite ses pavillons multicolores sous les brises du matin. J'ai créé toutes les fêtes, tous les triomphes, tous les drames. J'ai essayé d'inventer de nouvelles fleurs, de nouveaux astres, de nouvelles chairs, de nouvelles langues. J'ai cru acquérir des pouvoirs surnaturels. Et bien! je dois enterrer mon imagination et mes souvenirs! Une belle gloire d'artiste et de conteur emportée!

Moi! moi qui me suis dit mage ou ange, dispensé de toute morale, je suis rendu au sol, avec un devoir à chercher, et la réalité rugueuse à étreindre! Paysan!

Suis-je trompé? la charité serait-elle soeur de la mort pour moi?

Enfin, je demanderai pardon pour m'être nourri de mensonge. Et allons.

Mais pas une main amie! et où puiser le secours?

———

Oui, l'heure nouvelle est au moins très sévère.

Car je puis dire que la victoire m'est acquise: les grincements de dents, les sifflements de feu, les soupirs empestés se modèrent. Tous les souvenirs immondes s'effacent. Mes derniers regrets détalent,—des jalousies pour les mendiants, les brigands, les amis de la mort, les arriérés de toutes sortes.—Damnés, si je me vengeais.

Il faut être absolument moderne.

Autumn already!—But why regret an everlasting sun, since we're hell-bent on discovering divine light—far from those who die with the seasons.

Autumn. Our boat, lifting up in the motionless mists, turns towards the port of misery, the enormous city in a sky splotched with fire and muck. Ah, the rotten rags, the rain-soaked bread, the drunkenness, the thousand loves that've crucified me! She'll never be through, then, that ghoulish queen of a million dead souls and bodies *which are going to be judged!* I see myself again—skin eaten away by muck and plague, hair and armpits full of worms, and still much larger worms in the heart, bedding down with ageless, heartless strangers... I could've died there. . . . Ghastly memory! I loathe destitution.

And I dread winter because it's the cozy season!

—Sometimes in the sky I see limitless beaches covered with white countries full of joy. A huge golden ship, high above me, waves its many-colored banners in the morning breezes. I've created all the holidays, all the triumphs, all the dramas. I've tried to invent new flowers, new stars, new flesh, new tongues. I thought I'd acquired supernatural powers. Oh well! my imagination and my memories must be buried! A grrrrrreat artist's and story-teller's fame blinked out!

Me! me who's called myself magus and angel, above every moral code, I yield to the earth—there's duty to look for, there's a rugged reality to grasp! Peasant!

Was I wrong? Is charity death's kid sister for the likes of me?

Anyway, I'll ask forgiveness for having gorged myself on lies. Move along.

But not *one* friendly hand! and where do you turn for help. . . ?

Yes, the new hour's at least pretty harsh.

Because I can say victory's been won: the gnashing of teeth, the hissing of fire, the stinking sobs are simmering down. All the filthy memories are fading away. My last regrets scurry off—feeling jealous of beggars, of thieves, of death's friends, of the maladjusted of all kinds.—Damn! if I ever get revenge!

We've got to be strictly modern.

Point de cantiques: tenir le pas gagné. Dure nuit! le sang séché fume sur ma face, et je n'ai rien derrière moi, que cet horrible arbrisseau!... Le combat spirituel est aussi brutal que la bataille d'hommes; mais la vision de la justice est le plaisir de Dieu seul.

Cependant c'est la veille. Recevons tous les influx de vigueur et de tendresse réelle. Et à l'aurore, armés d'une ardente patience, nous entrerons aux splendides villes.

Que parlais-je de main amie! Un bel avantage, c'est que je puis rire des vieilles amours mensongères, et frapper de honte ces couples menteurs,—j'ai vu l'enfer des femmes là-bas;—et il me sera loisible de *posséder la vérité dans une âme et un corps.*

Avril-août, 1873.

No more canticles: hang on to what's been won. Hard night! dried blood smoking on my face, and I've got nothing behind me except that horrible bush. . . ! Spiritual combat's as brutal as battling with people, but the vision of justice is the pleasure of God alone.

But now it's the vigil. Let's welcome all the influx of vigor and genuine tenderness. And at dawn, armed with an ardent patience, we'll walk right into the magnificent cities.

Why talk about a friendly hand! One nice benefit is that now I can ridicule the old fakeries of love and heap scorn on all those two-faced couples—I saw the hell of women down there!—and now I'll be at liberty *to enjoy the whole truth in one soul and one body.*

April–August, 1873

ILLUMINATIONS

I

VIE DE L'ENFANT

LIFE OF THE CHILD

"We're in the months of love; I'm seventeen years old. The time of hopes and dreams, as they say—and here I am, getting started—a child touched by the finger of the Muse—excuse me if that's trite—to express my fine beliefs, my yearnings, my feelings, all those things poets know—myself, I call them spring things."

Letter to Théodore de Banville
(Charleville, May 1870)

APRÈS LE DÉLUGE

Aussitôt que l'idée du Déluge se fut rassise,

Un lièvre s'arrêta dans les sainfoins et les clochettes mouvantes et dit sa prière à l'arc-en-ciel à travers la toile de l'araignée.

Oh! les pierres précieuses qui se cachaient,—les fleurs qui regardaient déjà.

Dans la grande rue sale les étals se dressèrent, et l'on tira les barques vers la mer étagée là-haut comme sur les gravures.

Le sang coula, chez Barbe-Bleue,—aux abattoirs,—dans les cirques, où le sceau de Dieu blêmit les fenêtres. Le sang et le lait coulèrent.

Les castors bâtirent. Les «mazagrans» fumèrent dans les estaminets.

Dans la grande maison de vitres encore ruisselante les enfants en deuil regardèrent les merveilleuses images.

Une porte claqua,—et sur la place du hameau, l'enfant tourna ses bras, compris des girouettes et des coqs des clochers de partout, sous l'éclatante giboulée.

Madame *** établit un piano dans les Alpes. La messe et les premières communions se célèbrent aux cent mille autels de la cathédrale.

Les caravanes partirent. Et le Splendide-Hôtel fut bâti dans le chaos de glaces et nuit du pôle.

Depuis lors, la Lune entendit les chacals piaulant par les déserts de thym,—et les églogues en sabots grognant dans le verger. Puis, dans la futaie violette, bourgeonnante, Eucharis me dit que c'était le printemps.

Sourds, étang,—Écume, roule sur le pont et par-dessus les bois;—draps noirs et orgues,—éclairs et tonnerre,—montez et roulez;—Eaux et tristesses, montez et relevez les Déluges.

Car depuis qu'ils se sont dissipés,—oh les pierres précieuses s'enfouissant, et les fleurs ouvertes!—c'est un ennui! et la Reine, la Sorcière qui allume sa braise dans le pot de terre, ne voudra jamais nous raconter ce qu'elle sait, et que nous ignorons.

As soon as the idea of the Flood simmered down,

A rabbit stood still in the clover and swinging flowerbells, and said a prayer to the rainbow through the spider's web.

Oh! the priceless stones that were hiding—the flowers that were regaining their eyesight.

In the messy main street, display cases were being built and boats were being dragged to the sea piled high like in etchings.

The blood flowed at Bluebeard's—through the stockyards—at the circuses, wherever God's touch turned the windows white. Both blood and milk flowed.

Beavers kept building. Coffee pots kept steaming up the cafes.

In the big house with windowpanes still dripping, children in mourning were looking at the marvelous pictures.

A door crashed, and on the town parade ground, the boy waved his arms and was recognized right away by weathervanes and steeple cocks from all over in that crackling downpour.

Madam *** set up a piano in the Alps. Mass and first communions were being celebrated at the hundred thousand altars of the cathedral.

Motorcades were setting out. And the Hotel Splendid was built in the chaos of ice and the polar night.

Since then, the Moon has been hearing wild dogs howling in deserts of thyme—and eclogues in wooden shoes growling in the orchard. And now, in a budding grove crowded with violets, a eucharis tells me spring has come.

Flood, pond!—Foam, pour over the bridge and all over the woods. Dark organs and shrouds, thunder and lightning, *rise and roll!*—Waters and miseries, rise up and bring back more Floods.

Because since they disappeared—oh! the priceless stones being buried and the open flowers!—it's been a bore! and the Queen, the Witch that lights her fire in an earthenware bowl, won't ever tell us what she grasps, and what we'll never know.

J'ai embrassé l'aube d'été.

Rien ne bougeait encore au front des palais. L'eau était morte. Les camps d'ombres ne quittaient pas la route du bois. J'ai marché, réveillant les haleines vives et tièdes, et les pierreries regardèrent, et les ailes se levèrent sans bruit.

La première entreprise fut, dans le sentier déjà empli de frais et blêmes éclats, une fleur qui me dit son nom.

Je ris au wasserfall blond qui *s'échevela* à travers les sapins: à la cime argentée je reconnus la déesse.

Alors je levai un à un les voiles. Dans l'allée, en agitant les bras. Par la plaine, où je l'ai dénoncée au coq. À la grand'ville elle fuyait parmi les clochers et les dômes, et courant comme un mendiant sur les quais de marbre, je la chassais.

En haut de la route, près d'un bois de lauriers, je l'ai entourée avec ses voiles amassés, et j'ai senti un peu son immense corps. L'aube et l'enfant tombèrent au bas du bois.

Au réveil il était midi.

I've embraced the summer dawn.

Nothing budged yet on the walls of the palaces. The water was dead still. Camps of shadows held the road to the woods. I tramped on, waking up the lukewarm living breezes, and the stones watched, and wings were beating without sound.

The first real happening on the little path already filled with fresh pale flashings was a flower that told me its name.

I chuckled at the blond waterfall *disheveled* through the pine trees: at their silvered tips, I made out the goddess.

I started lifting her veils, one by one. In the path, by waving my arms. In the field, where I gave her away to the cock. All over town, she ran away between the steeples and domes, and, moving like a hustler on the piers of marble, I hassled her!

Where the road turns upwards, near a laurel wood, I bundled her all up in her veils, and I felt her huge body a bit. Dawn and the child dropped together at the wood's edge.

When I woke it was noon.

I

Cette idole, yeux noirs et crin jaune, sans parents ni cour, plus noble que la fable, mexicaine et flamande; son domaine, azur et verdure insolents, court sur des plages nommées, par des vagues sans vaisseaux, de noms férocement grecs, slaves, celtiques.

À la lisière de la forêt—les fleurs de rêve tintent, éclatent, éclairent,—la fille à lèvre d'orange, les genoux croisés dans le clair déluge qui sourd des prés, nudité qu'ombrent, traversent et habillent les arcs-en-ciel, la flore, la mer.

Dames qui tournoient sur les terrasses voisines de la mer; enfantes et géantes, superbes noires dans la mousse vert-de-gris, bijoux debout sur le sol gras des bosquets et des jardinets dégelés,—jeunes mères et grandes sœurs aux regards pleins de pèlerinages, sultanes, princesses de démarche et de costume tyranniques, petites étrangères et personnes doucement malheureuses.

Quel ennui, l'heure du «cher corps» et «cher cœur»!

II

C'est elle, la petite morte, derrière les rosiers.—La jeune maman trépassée descend le perron.—La calèche du cousin crie sur le sable.—Le petit frère (il est aux Indes!) là, devant le couchant, sur le pré d'œillets.—Les vieux qu'on a enterrés tout droits dans le rempart aux giroflées.

L'essaim des feuilles d'or entoure la maison du général. Ils sont dans le midi.—On suit la route rouge pour arriver à l'auberge vide. Le château est à vendre; les persiennes sont détachées.—Le curé aura emporté la clef de l'église.—Autour du parc, les loges des gardes sont inhabitées. Les palissades sont si hautes qu'on ne voit que les cimes bruissantes. D'ailleurs il n'y a rien à voir là-dedans.

Les prés remontent aux hameaux sans coqs, sans enclumes. L'écluse est levée. Ô les Calvaires et les moulins du désert, les îles et les meules!

CHILDHOOD

I

This idol, eyes black and yellow mane, no family and no following, but placed higher up than Mexican or Flemish fables; his turf, insolent blue and green, extends on boatless waves to beaches with names ferociously Greek, Slavic, Celtic.

At the wood's edge—dream-flowers buzz, flash, illuminate—the girl with orange lips, knees crossed in the clear flood springing up from the fields, her nakedness shadowed, penetrated, dressed up by rainbows, flora, sea.

Ladies walking around on balconies next to the sea; baby girls and she-giants, superb black women in gray-green foam, jewels erect in the rich soil of groves and little thawed gardens—young mothers and big sisters with eyes brimful of pilgrimages, sultans, princesses tyrannical in their stride and their get-up, little foreign girls and people mildly unhappy.

What a bore, the idea of "dear girl" and "dear heart."

II

It's her, the little dead girl, behind the rosebushes.—The young mother, also dead, walks down the steps.—The cousin's carriage creaks in the sand.—The little brother (he's in India!) right there, in front of the sunset, in the field of carnations.—The old men they've buried upright in the wall of gilly-flowers.

Swarms of gold leaves surround the general's house. They're in the south.—You follow the red road to reach the empty inn. The chateau's up for sale and the shutters are falling apart.—The priest must have spirited away the key to the church.—All over the grounds, the keepers' cabins are empty. The fences are so high, all you can see are the treetops blowing in the wind. Besides, there's nothing to see in there.

The fields are crowding in on these towns with no cocks and no anvils. The sluice gates are open. Oh the calvaries and the deserted blow mills, the islands and the haystacks!

Des fleurs magiques bourdonnaient. Les talus le berçaient. Des bêtes d'une élégance fabuleuse circulaient. Les nuées s'amassaient sur la haute mer faite d'une éternité de chaudes larmes.

III

Au bois il y a un oiseau, son chant vous arrête et vous fait rougir.
Il y a une horloge qui ne sonne pas.
Il y a une fondrière avec un nid de bêtes blanches.
Il y a une cathédrale qui descend et un lac qui monte.
Il y a une petite voiture abandonnée dans le taillis, ou qui descent le sentier en courant, enrubannée.
Il y a une troupe de petits comédiens en costumes, aperçus sur la route à travers la lisière du bois.
Il y a enfin, quand l'on a faim et soif, quelqu'un qui vous chasse.

IV

Je suis le saint, en prière sur la terrasse,—comme les bêtes pacifiques paissent jusqu'à la mer de Palestine.
Je suis le savant au fauteuil sombre. Les branches et la pluie se jettent à la croisée de la bibliothèque.
Je suis le piéton de la grand'route par les bois nains; la rumeur des écluses couvre mes pas. Je vois longtemps la mélancolique lessive d'or du couchant.
Je serais bien l'enfant abandonné sur la jetée partie à la haute mer, le petit valet suivant l'allée dont le front touche le ciel.
Les sentiers sont âpres. Les monticules se couvrent de genêts. L'air est immobile. Que les oiseaux et les sources sont loin! Ce ne peut être que la fin du monde, en avançant.

V

Qu'on me loue enfin ce tombeau, blanchi à la chaux avec les lignes du ciment en relief—très loin sous terre.

Magic flowers were buzzing. The slopes were rocking him. Fabulously gorgeous animals running around. Clouds were gathering over high seas made up of eternities of scalding tears.

III

In the woods there's a bird, his song stops you dead and makes you blush.

There's a clock that doesn't strike.

There's a quagmire with a nest of white animals.

There's a cathedral that goes down and a lake that comes up.

There's a little toy wagon ditched in the bushes, or, all covered with ribbons, zooming down the road.

There's a troupe of little actors in costumes, glimpsed on the road at the woods' edge.

And finally, when you get hungry and thirsty, there's someone there to hassle you.

IV

I'm the saint, in prayer on the balcony—just like the peace-loving animals that graze all the way to the sea of Palestine.

I'm the scholar in his dark easychair. The branches and the rain beat against the library windows.

I'm the hitchhiker on the highways that run through low woods. The roar of the sluices drowns out my steps. I look a long while at the depressing gold-smudged wash of the setting sun.

I could easily be the kid abandoned on a pier that's heading out for the high seas, the young farm hand following the trail whose upper reaches touch the sky.

The paths are rough. The knolls are covered with stubble. The air is motionless. How far-off are the birds and the springs! This has got to be the end of the world, this moving ahead.

V

Let them rent me this grave, insides whitewashed, with cement lines in relief—far down underground.

Je m'accoude à la table, la lampe éclaire très vivement ces journaux que je suis idiot de relire, ces livres sans intérêt.—

À une distance énorme au-dessus de mon salon souterrain, les maisons s'implantent, les brumes s'assemblent. La boue est rouge ou noire. Ville monstrueuse, nuit sans fin!

Moins haut, sont des égouts. Aux côtés, rien que l'épaisseur du globe. Peut-être les gouffres d'azur, des puits de feu. C'est peut-être sur ces plans que se rencontrent lunes et comètes, mers et fables.

Aux heures d'amertume je m'imagine des boules de saphir, de métal. Je suis maître du silence. Pourquoi une apparence de soupirail blêmirait-elle au coin de la voûte?

I lean my elbows on the table, the lamp shines brightly on these newspapers which I'm dumb enough to read again, these idiotic books.

At a tremendous distance over my underground living room, the houses sink roots, the fogs gather round. The muck is red or black. Nightmare city! Night without end.

Less high up are the sewers. Around me, only the thickness of the globe. Perhaps chasms of azure or deep wells of fire. Or perhaps at these levels comets and moons rendezvous, myths and seas.

In hours of bitterness, I imagine balls of sapphire, balls of metal. I'm master of silence. So why should the outlines of a vent begin to flash, faintly, at the corner of my ceiling?

JEUNESSE

I

DIMANCHE

Les calculs de côté, l'inévitable descente du ciel, et la visite des souvenirs et la séance des rythmes occupent la demeure, la tête et le monde de l'esprit.

—Un cheval détale sur le turf suburbain, et le long des cultures et des boisements, percé par la peste carbonique. Une misérable femme de drame, quelque part dans le monde, soupire après des abandons improbables. Les desperadoes languissent après l'orage, l'ivresse et les blessures. De petits enfants étouffent des malédictions le long des rivières.—

Reprenons l'étude au bruit de l'oeuvre dévorante qui se rassemble et remonte dans les masses.

II

SONNET

Homme de constitution ordinaire, la chair n'était-elle pas un fruit pendu dans le verger, ô journées enfantes! le corps un trésor à prodiguer; ô aimer, le péril ou la force de Psyché? La terre avait des versants fertiles en princes et en artistes, et la descendance et la race vous poussaient aux crimes et aux deuils: le monde votre fortune et votre péril. Mais à présent, ce labeur comblé, toi, tes calculs, toi, tes impatiences, ne sont plus que votre danse et votre voix, non fixées et point forcées, quoique d'un double événement d'invention et de succès une raison, en l'humanité fraternelle et discrète par l'univers sans images;—la force et le droit réfléchissent la danse et la voix à présent seulement appréciées.

YOUTH

I

SUNDAY

When schoolwork's set aside, the inevitable descent of the blue and return of memories and the stilling of rhythms become the concerns of family life, the head, and the realm of the spirit.

—A horse scampers off on the suburban turf, along the gardens and wood lots, nauseated by the carbonic plague. Somewhere in the world, a miserable histrionic woman is sighing for unlikely desertions. Desperados are just dying for scraps, or drunkenness, or wounds. Along the rivers little children are choking on their own blasphemies.—

Let's get back to studies in the midst of the thundering task that's regrouping and rising in the masses.

II

SONNET

Man of ordinary constitution, wasn't the flesh a fruit hanging in the orchard? Oh days of childhood!—the body a treasure to squander? Oh to love, the danger or power of Psyche? The earth had slopes fertile with princes and artists, and ancestry and race drove you to crimes and to mourning: the world, your fortune and your peril. But now that this work's completed, you, your scheming, you, your impatiences, are merely your dance and your voice, not fixed and not forced, although the reason for the twofold achievement of invention and success is here: in a mankind both separate and together, filling an imageless universe—might and right both echoing your dance and your voice, only now appreciated. . . .

III

Les voix instructives exilées... L'ingénuité physique amèrement rassise... Adagio. Ah! l'égoïsme infini de l'adolescence, l'optimisme studieux: que le monde était plein de fleurs cet été! Les airs et les formes mourant... Un chœur, pour calmer l'impuissance et l'absence! Un chœur de verres, de mélodies nocturnes... En effet les nerfs vont vite chasser.

IV

Tu en es encore à la tentation d'Antoine. L'ébat du zèle écourté, les tics d'orgueil puéril, l'affaissement et l'effroi.

Mais tu te mettras à ce travail: toutes les possibilités harmoniques et architecturales s'émouvront autour de ton siège. Des êtres parfaits, imprévus, s'offriront à tes expériences. Dans tes environs affluera rêveusement la curiosité d'anciennes foules et de luxes oisifs. Ta mémoire et tes sens ne seront que la nourriture de ton impulsion créatrice. Quant au monde, quand tu sortiras, que sera-t-il devenu? En tout cas, rien des apparences actuelles.

III

The teaching voices exiled. . . . Physical candor bitterly slapped
down. . . . Adagio. Ah! the limitless egotism of adolescence, the
studious optimism: how the world was full of flowers that summer!
Melodies and forms dying out. . . . A choir, to calm down impotence
and absence! All right, the nerves go quickly beserk.

IV

You're still at St.Anthony's temptation. The bout with diminished
zeal, the tics of boyish pride, the collapse and the dread.

But you're going to get to work: all harmonic and architectonic pos-
sibilities will surge around your seat. Perfect beings, unimaginable, will
offer themselves to you to experiment with. All around you the
curiousity of ancient crowds and idle wealth will dreamily flow in.
Your memory and your senses will merely serve to feed your creative
impulses. As for the world, what's going to become of it after you've
gone? Anyway, not a trace of its current appearances.

Enfant, certains ciels ont affiné mon optique: tous les caractères nuancèrent ma physionomie. Les Phénomènes s'émurent.—À présent l'inflexion éternelle des moments et l'infini des mathématiques me chassent par ce monde où je subis tous les succès civils, respecté de l'enfance étrange et des affections énormes.—Je songe à une Guerre, de droit ou de force, de logique bien imprévue.

C'est aussi simple qu'une phrase musicale.

As a child, my eyesight was sharpened by certain skies: their features nuanced my whole appearance. The Phenomena came alive!— Right now, the endless inflections of moments and the infinity of mathematics are tracking me down all over this world in which I put up with civic acclaim, famous among weird kids and crushing displays of feeling.—I dream of a War, of right or of might, of unthinkable logic.

It's as simple as a musical phrase.

Se peut-il qu'Elle me fasse pardonner les ambitions continuellement écrasées,—qu'une fin aisée répare les âges d'indigence,—qu'un jour de succès nous endorme sur la honte de notre inhabileté fatale?

(Ô palmes! diamant!—Amour, force!—plus haut que toutes joies et gloires!—de toutes façons, partout,—démon, dieu,—Jeunesse de cet être-ci: moi!)

Que des accidents de féerie scientifique et des mouvements de fraternité sociale soient chéris comme restitution progressive de la franchise première?...

Mais la Vampire qui nous rend gentils commande que nous nous amusions avec ce qu'elle nous laisse, ou qu'autrement nous soyons plus drôles.

Rouler aux blessures, par l'air lassant et la mer; aux supplices, par le silence des eaux et de l'air meurtriers; aux tortures qui rient, dans leur silence atrocement houleux.

ANGUISH

Can it be that She'll have me acquitted for ambitions consistently squelched?—that wealth in the end will make up for years of privation?—that one day's success will wipe out the memory of my fatal lack of skill?

(O palms! diamonds!—Love, strength!—greater than all joys and all fame!—in every way, everywhere,—demon and god.—Seedtime of this being: me!)

That the accidents of scientific magic and the movement for social equality will be appreciated as the progressive restitution to our earliest freedom... ?

But the Vampire that makes us behave orders us to play with what she leaves us, or otherwise be more amusing.

Wrapped up in my wounds, through the tiresome air and the sea; in my torments, through the silence of waters and cutthroat air; in tortures that laugh out loud, in their crushing heaves of silence.

DÉMOCRATIE

«Le drapeau va au paysage immonde, et notre patois étouffe le tambour.

«Aux centres nous alimenterons la plus cynique prostitution. Nous massacrerons les révoltes logiques.

«Aux pays poivrés et détrempés!—au service des plus monstrueuses exploitations industrielles ou militaires.

«Au revoir ici, n'importe où. Conscrits du bon vouloir, nous aurons la philosophie féroce; ignorants pour la science, roués pour le confort; la crevaison pour le monde qui va. C'est la vraie marche. En avant, route!»

DEMOCRACY

"The flag's taking off for that filthy place, and our jargon's drowning out the drums.

"In the big cities, we'll keep alive an all-out cynical whoring. We'll massacre all revolts that make sense.

"On to the wasted and dried-up countries!—at the service of the most monstrously efficient military-industrial complexes.

"Goodbye to here, forget what's there. Recruits of good will, we'll have a ferocious philosophy. Not caring for science, eager for comforts—let the rest of the world go blow! This is the real thing. For-waaaaard, *march!*"

H

Toutes les monstruosités violent les gestes atroces d'Hortense. Sa solitude est la mécanique érotique, sa lassitude, la dynamique amoureuse. Sous la surveillance d'une enfance elle a été, à des époques nombreuses, l'ardente hygiène des races. Sa porte est ouverte à la misère. Là, la moralité des êtres actuels se décorpore en sa passion ou en son action—Ô terrible frisson des amours novices sur le sol sanglant et par l'hydrogène clarteux! trouvez Hortense.

H

All these monstrosities are ravishing Hortense's heartless dumb show. Her loneliness means erotic mechanics; her lassitude, the dynamics of love. On the proving ground of childhood, she's often been the grabbed-at hygiene of the races. Her door's wide open to impoverishment. There, the morals of living beings are disembodied in her passion or her action.—O awful shudderings of novice love on the bleeding floor, in the transfigured air!—locate Hortense.

VIE DU POÈTE

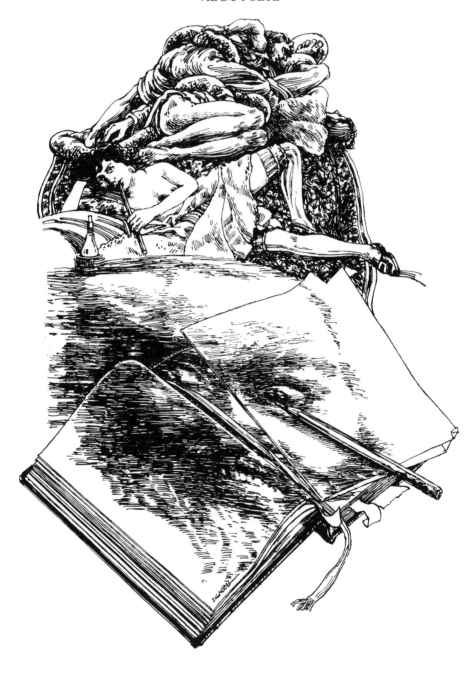

II

LIFE OF THE POET

"The sufferings are enormous, but one has to be tough, one has to be born a poet, and I've come to realize I'm a poet. It's not at all my fault. It's wrong to say: I think. One has to say: I am thought... I is another. Too bad for the wood that finds itself a violin, and to hell with the unaware who babble and crackle about things they can't understand at all!"

Letter to Georges Izambard
(Charleville, May 1871)

Un Prince était vexé de ne s'être employé jamais qu'à la perfection des générosités vulgaires. Il prévoyait d'étonnantes révolutions de l'amour, et soupçonnait ses femmes de pouvoir mieux que cette complaisance agrémentée de ciel et de luxe. Il voulait voir la vérité, l'heure du désir et de la satisfaction essentiels. Que ce fût ou non une aberration de piété, il voulut. Il possédait au moins un assez large pouvoir humain.

Toutes les femmes qui l'avaient connu furent assassinées. Quel saccage du jardin de la beauté! Sous le sabre, elles le bénirent. Il n'en commanda point de nouvelles.—Les femmes réapparurent.

Il tua tous ceux qui le suivaient, après la chasse ou les libations.—Tous le suivaient.

Il s'amusa à égorger les bêtes de luxe. Il fit flamber les palais. Il se ruait sur les gens et les taillait en pièces.—La foule, les toits d'or, les belles bêtes existaient encore.

Peut-on s'extasier dans la destruction, se rajeunir par la cruauté! Le peuple ne murmura pas. Personne n'offrit le concours de ses vues.

Un soir il galopait fièrement. Un Génie apparut, d'une beauté ineffable, inavouable même. De sa physionomie et de son maintien ressortait la promesse d'un amour multiple et complexe! d'un bonheur indicible, insupportable même! Le Prince et le Génie s'anéantirent probablement dans la santé essentielle. Comment n'auraient-ils pas pu en mourir? Ensemble donc ils moururent.

Mais ce Prince décéda, dans son palais, à un âge ordinaire. Le Prince était le Génie. Le Génie était le Prince.

La musique savante manque à notre désir.

A Prince was sick and tired of having wasted so much of his time practicing the customary courtesies. He could foresee astonishing revolutions of love and suspected his women of being able to give much more than their complacencies, compounded of air and luxury. He wanted to see the truth, the hour of essential desire and satisfaction! Even at the risk of overdoing devotion, that's what he wanted. At least he had a rather large supply of mortal spunk.

All the women who had known him had to die. What slaughter in the garden of beauty! They all blessed him as the sword descended down. He didn't order any new ones.—The women reappeared.

He killed all those who followed him, after hunting or drinking bouts.—Everyone followed him.

He amused himself slitting the throats of really costly beasts. He set fire to palaces. He hurled himself on people and hacked them to pieces.—The crowds, the golden rooftops, the beautiful beasts went on existing.

Can a person know ecstasy in destruction, rejuvenation in cruelty? The people didn't complain. No one offered the benefit of his views.

One night he was horseback-riding, really cocky. A Genie appeared, incredibly beautiful, unspeakably even. His face and his bearing glowed with the promise of a love both many-sided and complicated! of an indescribable happiness, unbearable even! The Prince and the Genie killed each other, most probably in essential health. How could they help dying of it? Together then they died.

But this Prince died in his palace at the customary age. The Prince was the Genie. The Genie was the Prince.

Our desires still lack a cunning music.

PARADE

Des drôles très solides. Plusieurs ont exploité vos mondes. Sans besoins, et peu pressés de mettre en oeuvre leurs brillantes facultés et leur expérience de vos consciences. Quels hommes mûrs! Des yeux hébétés à la façon de la nuit d'été, rouges et noirs, tricolores, d'acier piqué d'étoiles d'or; des facies déformés, plombés, blêmis, incendiés; des enrouements folâtres! La démarche cruelle des oripeaux!—Il y a quelques jeunes,—comment regarderaient-ils Chérubin?—pourvus de voix effrayantes et de quelques ressources dangereuses. On les envoie prendre du dos en ville, affublés d'un *luxe* dégoûtant.

Ô le plus violent Paradis de la grimace enragée! Pas de comparaison avec vos Fakirs et les autres bouffonneries scéniques. Dans des costumes improvisés avec le goût du mauvais rêve ils jouent des complaintes, des tragédies de malandrins et de demi-dieux spirituels comme l'histoire ou les religions ne l'ont jamais été. Chinois, Hottentots, bohémiens, niais, hyènes, Molochs, vieilles démences, démons sinistres, ils mêlent les tours populaires, maternels, avec les poses et les tendresses bestiales. Ils interpréteraient des pièces nouvelles et des chansons «bonnes filles». Maîtres jongleurs, ils transforment le lieu et les personnes et usent de la comédie magnétique. Les yeux flambent, le sang chante, les os s'élargissent, les larmes et des filets rouges ruissellent. Leur raillerie ou leur terreur dure une minute, ou des mois entiers.

J'ai seul la clef de cette parade sauvage.

Tough customers. Many of them exploited your worlds. Needing nothing at all, and in no hurry to make use of their brilliant faculties and their experience of your tender consciences. Pretty virile men! Eyes listless like a summer night, reddened and blackish, three-shaded, steel studded with yellow stars. Features twisted, leaden, bloodless, gutted. Moronic hoarsenesses! The merciless posturings of tinsel! — Some are young guys—what would they think of Cherubino?—with bloodcurdling voices and some pretty dangerous equipment. They send these studs to town to bugger, decked out in disgusting clothes.

O the more violent Kingdom Come of the raging smirk! No comparison with your Fakirs and other stage antics. In costumes improvised with the taste of bad dreams, they act out sad songs and tragedies of thieves and demigods more uplifting than history or religion has ever managed to be! Chinese, Hottentots, gypsies, nitwits, hyenas, Molochs, old lunacies, sinister demons, they mix much-loved oldtime ditties meant for Mom with bestial winks and caresses. They're authorities on new pieces for the stage and tunes about "fair lassies." Master stuntsmen, they can transform both the scene and the characters: they use magnetic tricks. Eyes glisten, blood sings, bones grow bigger, tears and little red lines glow. Their horseplay or their panic terror may last a minute, or whole months.

I alone have the key to this screwy side show.

ANTIQUE

Gracieux Fils de Pan! Autour de ton front couronné de fleurettes et de baies, tes yeux, des boules précieuses, remuent. Tachées de lies brunes, tes joues se creusent. Tes crocs luisent. Ta poitrine ressemble à une cithare, des tintements circulent dans tes bras blonds. Ton coeur bat dans ce ventre où dort le double sexe. Promène-toi, la nuit, en mouvant doucement cette cuisse, cette seconde cuisse et cette jambe de gauche.

ANTIQUE

Gorgeous son of Pan! Beneath your brow crowned with flowers and berries, your eyes, these precious balls, move around. Streaked with coarse brown, your cheeks look hollow. Your fangs gleam. Your chest looks like a lyre, jingling sounds are moving in your blond arms. Your heart's beating in this belly where the double sex sleeps. Walk around, at night, slowly moving this thigh, then this other thigh, and this left leg.

La réalité étant trop épineuse pour mon grand caractère,—je me trouvai néanmoins chez Madame, en gros oiseau gris bleu s'essorant vers les moulures du plafond et traînant l'aile dans les ombres de la soirée.

Je fus, au pied du baldaquin supportant ses bijoux adorés et ses chefs-d'oeuvre physiques, un gros ours aux gencives violettes et au poil chenu de chagrin, les yeux aux cristaux et aux argents des consoles.

Tout se fit ombre et aquarium ardent. Au matin,—aube de juin batailleuse,—je courus aux champs, âne, claironnant et brandissant mon grief, jusqu'à ce que les Sabines de la banlieue vinrent se jeter à mon poitrail.

BOTTOM

Reality being too prickly for my famous character,—I found myself nevertheless at my lady's, in the shape of a huge gray-blue bird soaring toward the moldings of the ceiling and dragging my wings across the shadows of the evening.

At the foot of the canopy supporting her adored jewels and her physical masterpieces, I was a large bear with purplish gums and a fur thick with misery, eyes of crystal and silver from the consoles.

All things turned dark and ardent aquarium. In the morning— aggressive dawn of June—I ran to the fields, ass, braying and brandishing my grief, until the Sabine women of the suburbs came and hurled themselves at my torso.

Devant une neige, un Être de Beauté de haute taille. Des sifflements de mort et des cercles de musique sourde font monter, s'élargir et trembler comme un spectre ce corps adoré; des blessures écarlates et noires éclatent dans les chairs superbes. Les couleurs propres de la vie se foncent, dansent, et se dégagent autour de la Vision, sur le chantier. Et les frissons s'élèvent et grondent, et la saveur forcenée de ces effets se chargeant avec les sifflements mortels et les rauques musiques que le monde, loin derrière nous, lance sur notre mère de beauté,—elle recule, elle se dresse. Oh! nos os sont revêtus d'un nouveau corps amoureux.

O la face cendrée, l'écusson de crin, les bras de cristal! Le canon sur lequel je dois m'abattre à travers la mêlée des arbres et de l'air léger!

Against some snow, a Beautiful Being exquisitely tall. Whistlings of death and rings of unheard music make this adored body grow taller, spring outward, and shiver like a phantom; reddish and blackish wounds break open in the superb flesh. The colors of life itself deepen, dance, and drift around this Vision, on display in the yard. Shivers rise and rumble, and the frenetic taste of these effects clashes with the mortal whistlings, and the raucous music which the world, far beneath us, hurls at our mother of beauty—she backs up, she rears up. Oh! our bones are dressed again in our new amorous bodies!

O the ashen face, the horsehair escutcheon, the slippery limbs! The awesome leg-bone I've got to come sliding down through this medley of trees and nimble breezes!

L'ancienne Comédie poursuit ses accords et divise ses Idylles:

Des boulevards de tréteaux,

Un long pier en bois d'un bout à l'autre d'un champ rocailleux où la foule barbare évolue sous les arbres dépouillés.

Dans des corridors de gaze noire, suivant le pas des promeneurs aux lanternes et aux feuilles.

Des oiseaux des mystères s'abattent sur un ponton de maçonnerie mû par l'archipel couvert des embarcations des spectateurs.

Des scènes lyriques accompagnées de flûte et de tambour s'inclinent dans des réduits ménagés sous les plafonds, autour des salons de clubs modernes ou des salles de l'Orient ancien.

La féerie manoeuvre au sommet d'un amphithéâtre couronné par les taillis,—ou s'agite et module pour les Béotiens, dans l'ombre des futaies mouvantes sur l'arête des cultures.

L'opéra-comique se divise sur notre scène à l'arête d'intersection de dix cloisons dressées de la galerie aux feux.

The ancient Comedy seeks its agreements and divides its Idylls:
Boulevards of stages.

A long wooden pier from one end of a rocky field to another, where
the barbaric mob shoves forward under bare trees.

In hallways of black gauze, following in the footsteps of the strollers
among lanterns and leaves.

Birds out of plays fly down to a concrete pontoon moved by the cov-
ered archipelago of spectators coming aboard.

Lyric scenes, accompanied by flute and drum, bend down from nar-
rowing corners around the ceilings of modern clubs or halls of the an-
cient Orient.

The fairy-play is put on at the summit of an amphitheater crowned
with thick shrubs—or noisily and gently for the Beotians in the shade
of wind-blown trees at the edge of the gardens.

The comic opera is broken up on our stage at the intersecting line of
ten partitions set up from gallery to footlights.

VIES

I

Ô les énormes avenues du pays saint, les terrasses du temple! Qu'a-t-on fait du brahmane qui m'expliqua les Proverbes? D'alors, de là-bas, je vois encore même les vieilles! Je me souviens des heures d'argent et de soleil vers les fleuves, la main de la campagne sur mon épaule, et de nos caresses debout dans les plaines poivrées.—Un envol de pigeons écarlates tonne autour de ma pensée.—Exilé ici, j'ai eu une scène où jouer les chef-d'oeuvre dramatiques de toutes les littératures. Je vous indiquerais les richesses inouïes. J'observe l'histoire des trésors que vous trouvâtes. Je vois la suite! Ma sagesse est aussi dédaignée que le chaos. Qu'est mon néant, auprès de la stupeur qui vous attend?

II

Je suis un inventeur bien autrement méritant que tous ceux qui m'ont précédé; un musicien même, qui ai trouvé quelque chose comme la clef de l'amour. À présent, gentilhomme d'une campagne aigre au ciel sobre, j'essaye de m'émouvoir au souvenir de l'enfance mendiante, de l'apprentissage ou de l'arrivée en sabots, des polémiques, des cinq ou six veuvages, et quelques noces où ma forte tête m'empêcha de monter au diapason des camarades. Je ne regrette pas ma vieille part de gaîté divine: l'air sobre de cette aigre campagne alimente fort activement mon atroce scepticisme. Mais comme ce scepticisme ne peut désormais être mis en oeuvre, et que d'ailleurs je suis dévoué à un trouble nouveau,—j'attends de devenir un très méchant fou.

LIVES

I

O the tremendous roadways of the holy land, the temple terraces! What's become of the Brahmin who taught me the Proverbs? I can still see even the old women of that time, of that place! I remember hours full of silver and sunshine near rivers, the touch of the countryside on my shoulder, and our caresses as we stood in the riddled fields.—A flight of blood-red pigeons thunders over my thoughts.—In that exile, I had a stage where I could act out all the world's dramatic literature. I could treat you to riches unheard of. I take note of the history of treasure you discovered. I see what's coming! My wisdom is as much disdained as chaos. What's my nothingness compared to the numbness that awaits you?

II

I'm an inventor far more deserving than all those preceding me—a musician who's found something like the key of love, in fact. For the time being, I'm a blueblood from a bleak land in dark times, I'm trying to get high by remembering my hustling childhood: learning the ropes, or getting there in wooden shoes, or the hassles, or the five or six split-ups, or several all-out gang-bangs when my level head saved me from freaking out like my buddies. I don't regret my share in those divine romps long ago: the bleak air of that landscape's darkness actively nourishes my brutal skepticism. But since this skepticism can no longer be played out, and that anyhow I'm given over to a new disorder,—I wait to turn into a very fiendish madman.

III

Dans un grenier où je fus enfermé à douze ans j'ai connu le monde, j'ai illustré la comédie humaine. Dans un cellier j'ai appris l'histoire. À quelque fête de nuit dans une cité du Nord, j'ai rencontré toutes les femmes des anciens peintres. Dans un vieux passage à Paris on m'a enseigné les sciences classiques. Dans une magnifique demeure cernée par l'Orient entier j'ai accompli mon immense oeuvre et passé mon illustre retraite. J'ai brassé mon sang. Mon devoir m'est remis. Il ne faut même plus songer à cela. Je suis réellement d'outre-tombe, et pas de commissions.

III

In an attic where I was locked up when I was twelve, I got acquainted with the world. I illustrated the human comedy. In a wine cellar, I learned history. At a night-long carouse in a northern city, I bumped into the women of all the old painters. In an old back-alley in Paris, I was taught the classical sciences. In a magnificent dwelling surrounded by the entire Orient, I succeeded in my prodigious work and earned a well-deserved retirement. I pushed my own blood. Now my work is over. I musn't even think of that any more. I'm really six feet under, so no special orders!

Quand le monde sera réduit en un seul bois noir pour nos quatre yeux étonnés,—en une plage pour deux enfants fidèles,—en une maison musicale pour notre claire sympathie,—je vous trouverai.

Qu'il n'y ait ici-bas qu'un vieillard seul, calme et beau, entouré d'un «luxe inouï»,—et je suis à vos genoux.

Que j'aie réalisé tous vos souvenirs,—que je sois celle qui sais vous garrotter,—je vous étoufferai.

———————

Quand nous sommes très forts,—qui recule? très gais,—qui tombe de ridicule? Quand nous sommes très méchants,—que ferait-on de nous?

Parez-vous, dansez, riez.—Je ne pourrai jamais envoyer l'Amour par la fenêtre.

———————

—Ma camarade, mendiante, enfant monstre! comme ça t'est égal, ces malheureuses et ces manoeuvres, et mes embarras. Attache-toi à nous avec ta voix impossible, ta voix! unique flatteur de ce vil désespoir.

———————

Une matinée couverte, en Juillet. Un goût de cendres vole dans l'air;—une odeur de bois suant dans l'âtre,—les fleurs rouies—le saccage des promenades—la bruine des canaux par les champs—pourquoi pas déjà les joujoux et l'encens?

———————

J'ai tendu des cordes de clocher à clocher; des guirlandes de fenêtre à fenêtre; des chaînes d'or d'étoile à étoile, et je danse.

———————

Le haut étang fume continuellement. Quelle sorcière va se dresser sur le couchant blanc? Quelles violettes frondaisons vont descendre?

———————

SPELLS

When the world's nothing but one dark wood for our four scared eyes—a beach for two faithful children—a musical house for our clear sympathy—I'll find you.

When there's only one old man left on earth, quiet and beautiful, living among "unheard of luxuries"—I'll be at your feet.

When I'm familiar with all your memories—when I'm the one who knows how to garrotte you—I'll strangle you.

———————

When we're very strong, who backs up? very happy,—who dies of shyness? When we're very bad,—what will they do with us?

Dress up, dance, laugh. I'll never want to toss Love out the window.

———————

My little buddy, hustler-girl, monstrous brat! these sexy wiles and my bashfulness are all the same to you. Hang on to us with your unbelievable voice, your voice! sole sycophant of this vile despair.

———————

Overcast morning, in July. A taste of ashes floats in the air;—the smell of sweaty wood in the fireplace,—soaking flowers,—garbage all over the sidewalks,—drizzle from the canals above the fields—why not playthings right now, and incense?

———————

I've stretched some ropes from belfry to belfry, garlands from window to window, gold chains from star to star, and I dance.

———————

The high pond is streaming endlessly. What witch will fly high over the white sunset? What purple fronds will come down?

———————

Pendant que les fonds publics s'écoulent en fêtes de fraternité, il sonne une cloche de feu rose dans les nuages.

―――――――――

Avivant un agréable goût d'encre de Chine, une poudre noire pleut doucement sur ma veillée.—Je baisse les feux du lustre, je me jette sur le lit, et tourné du côté de l'ombre je vous vois, mes filles! mes reines!

While public moneys are being squandered on "fraternal banquets," a bell of pink fire is ringing in the clouds.

———————

Rekindling a pleasant taste for China ink, a black powder rains softly on my evening. I lower the jets of the gaslights, I throw myself on the bed and, turning my face toward the dark, I see you, my girls! my queens!

Ô *mon* Bien! O *mon* Beau! Fanfare atroce où je ne trébuche point! Chevalet féerique! Hourra pour l'oeuvre inouïe et pour le corps merveilleux, pour la première fois! Cela commença sous les rires des enfants, cela finira par eux. Ce poison va rester dans toutes nos veines même quand, la fanfare tournant, nous serons rendus à l'ancienne inharmonie. Ô maintenant, nous si digne des ces tortures! rassemblons fervemment cette promesse surhumaine faite à notre corps et à notre âme créés: cette promesse, cette démence! L'élégance, la science, la violence! On nous a promis d'enterrer dans l'ombre l'arbre du bien et du mal, de déporter les honnêtetés tyranniques, afin que nous amenions notre très pur amour. Cela commença par quelques dégoûts et cela finit,—ne pouvant nous saisir sur-le-champ de cette éternité,— cela finit par une débandade de parfums.

Rire des enfants, discrétion des esclaves, austérité des vierges, horreur des figures et des objets d'ici, sacrés soyez-vous par le souvenir de cette veille. Cela commençait par toute la rustrerie, voici que cela finit par des anges de flamme et de glace.

Petite veille d'ivresse, sainte! quand ce ne serait que pour le masque dont tu nous as gratifié. Nous t'affirmons, méthode! Nous n'oublions pas que tu as glorifié hier chacun de nos âges. Nous avons foi au poison. Nous savons donner notre vie tout entière tous les jours.

Voici le temps des Assassins.

Oh *my* Good! Oh, *my* Beauty! Mind-blowing jive that won't mess with my footwork! cool torture, *far out!* Let's hear it for the good shit they can't hear and for the luscious body, this first time around! It's when kids died laughing these things started, and that's the way they'll end. It's a poison the blood gets hooked on, for good, even when your music's been zilched and you're into the old-time jazz again. So now that we're really digging this badass, let's come out and demand action on that hyped-up promise they made our souls and bodies in their famous long ago: their promise, their mind-blow—Elegance, Violence, and Science! They were going to do some pruning on the tree of good and evil, right? It began just a bit disgusting and it ended—since we weren't quite quick enough to clinch our fabulous beat—it ended in the smells of stampede.

Kids who can laugh, slaves still up-tight, virgins now cooling it, faces and things made uglier by this place, keep in mind we were free for a spell, we're all holy! It started with outright trickery, but look how it's ending with angels of fire and ice!

Brief days being high. HOLY! if only because of the masks you taught us how to wear. We accept you, technique! We're flashing back to the brightness you gave to each of those days. The future's here—we trust in poison. We're going the whole distance from here on out.

Now's the time of the *ASSASSINS.*

Pitoyable frère! Que d'atroces veillées je lui dus! «Je ne me saisissais pas fervemment de cette entreprise. Je m'étais joué de son infirmité. Par ma faute nous retournerions en exil, en esclavage.» Il me supposait un guignon et une innocence très bizarres, et il ajoutait des raisons inquiétantes.

Je répondais en ricanant à ce satanique docteur, et finissais par gagner la fenêtre. Je créais, par delà la campagne traversée par des bandes de musique rare, les fantômes du futur luxe nocturne.

Après cette distraction vaguement hygiénique, je m'étendais sur une paillasse. Et, presque chaque nuit, aussitôt endormi, le pauvre frère se levait, la bouche pourrie, les yeux arrachés,—tel qu'il se rêvait!—et me tirait dans la salle en hurlant son songe de chagrin idiot.

J'avais en effet, en toute sincérité d'esprit, pris l'engagement de le rendre à son état primitif de fils du Soleil,—et nous errions, nourris du vin des cavernes et du biscuit de la route, moi pressé de trouver le lieu et la formule.

Miserable brother! what atrocious nights I owed him! "I didn't put much passion into this affair. I simply played on his weakness. It's my fault if we go back into exile, into slavery." He figured I was jinxed and so queerly innocent, and he added worrisome reasons.

I'd answer this satanic doctor with a jeer, and would inch over to the window. I'd project, all over a landscape filled with strips of odd music, phantasms of sensuous nights to come.

After this vaguely hygienic distraction, I'd stretch on a straw mat. And almost every night, as soon as I'd fall asleep, the poor brother would get up, his mouth all dry and his eyes bulging out—just as he'd dreamed!—and would drag me into his room yowling his cock-eyed dream of misery.

I'd made a vow, in absolute sincerity, to bring him back again to his primitive state of son of the Sun—and we drifted, kept alive by the wine of dank dives and the dry bread of the road, myself all on fire to find the place and the formula.

VIE DANS LA NATURE

III

LIFE IN NATURE

"The provinces, where people feed on flour and mud, where they drink the local wine and the local beer, that's not what I miss. You're quite right to go on putting them down. But this place: distillation, composition, all narrowness: and the suffocating summer: the heat's not constant, but seeing that fine weather is in everybody's interest and that everyone is a pig, I hate summer which kills me even when it appears a little while. I'm as thirsty as a man with gangrene: the Belgian and Ardennes rivers and caves, *that's* what I miss."

Letter to Ernest Delahaye
(Paris, June 1872)

NOCTURNE VULGAIRE

Un souffle ouvre des brèches opéradiques dans les cloisons,—brouille de pivotement des toits rongés,—disperse les limites des foyers,—éclipse les croisées.—

Le long de la vigne, m'étant appuyé du pied à une gargouille,—je suis descendu dans ce carrosse dont l'époque est assez indiquée par les glaces convexes, les panneaux bombés et les sophas contournés. Corbillard de mon sommeil, isolé, maison de berger de ma niaiserie, le véhicule vire sur le gazon de la grande route effacée: et dans un défaut en haut de la glace de droite tournoient les blêmes figures lunaires, feuilles, seins!

—Un vert et un bleu très foncés envahissent l'image. Dételage aux environs d'une tache de gravier.

—Ici va-t-on siffler pour l'orage, et les Sodomes et les Solymes, et les bêtes féroces et les armées.

—(Postillon et bêtes de songe reprendront-ils sous les plus suffocantes futaies, pour m'enfoncer jusqu'aux yeux dans la source de soie?)

—Et nous envoyer, fouettés à travers les eaux clapotantes et les boissons répandues, rouler sur l'aboi des dogues...

—Un souffle disperse les limites du foyer.

A mere breath makes operatic cracks in the partitions—blurs the gyrations of the termite-eaten roofs—scatters the fireplace walls—wipes out the windows.—

After firmly steadying one foot on a gargoyle, I climbed down the vines to this coach, the era of which is clearly enough indicated by its convex windowpanes, its bulging sides, and its contorted seats. Hearse of my sleep, all by itself, shepherd's hut of my silliness, the vehicle turns around on the grass of the vanished highway: and in a defect in the top right-hand windowpane, pale moon figures, leaves, and tits spin!

A very deep green and blue invade the picture. Unhitching in the vicinity of a bit of gravel.

—Here we'll whistle for the storm, for Sodoms and Solymas, and for wild beasts and armies.

—(Will the conductor and dream animals in the suffocating woods start all over and plunge me up to my eyes in the fountain of silk?)

—And send us, whipped by swishing waters and spilled drinks, rolling on the yawping of bulldogs. . . .

—A mere breath scatters the fireplace walls.

D'un gradin d'or,—parmi les cordons de soie, les gazes grises, les velours verts et les disques de cristal qui noircissent comme du bronze au soleil,—je vois la digitale s'ouvrir sur un tapis de filigranes d'argent, d'yeux et de chevelures.

Des pièces d'or jaune semées sur l'agate, des piliers d'acajou supportant un dôme d'émeraudes, des bouquets de satin blanc et de fines verges de rubis entourent la rose d'eau.

Tels qu'un dieu aux énormes yeux bleus et aux formes de neige, la mer et le ciel attirent aux terrasses de marbre la foule des jeunes et fortes roses.

FLOWERS

From a gold step—among silk cords, gray gauzes, green velvets, and crystal discs that blacken like bronze in the sun—I see the foxglove opening up on a tapestry of silver filigree and eyes and heads of hair.

Coins of bright gold scattered on agate, mahogany columns supporting a dome of emeralds, bouquets of white satin and delicate inlays of rubies surround the waterrose.

Like a god with huge blue eyes and limbs like blizzards, the sky and sea entice to the marble stairway whole mobs of brash young roses.

MARINE

Les chars d'argent et de cuivre—
Les proues d'acier et d'argent—
Battent l'écume,—
Soulèvent les souches des ronces.
Les courants de la lande,
Et les ornières immenses du reflux,
Filent circulairement vers l'est,
Vers les piliers de la forêt,—
Vers les fûts de la jetée,
Dont l'angle est heurté par des tourbillons de lumière.

SEASCAPE

Machines of silver and copper—
Prows of steel and silver—
Threshing the foam,—
Turning over stumps of bramble.
The currents of the dunes,
The immense ruts of the ebb tide
Flowing circularly toward the East
Toward the pylons of the forest,—
Toward the timbers of the pier
Against whose boards whirlpools of daylight blow!

FÊTE D'HIVER

La cascade sonne derrière les huttes d'opéra-comique. Des girandoles prolongent, dans les vergers et les allées voisins du Méandre,—les verts et les rouges du couchant. Nymphes d'Horace coiffées au Premier Empire,—Rondes Sibériennes, Chinoises de Boucher.

The waterfall makes a noise behind the boxes of the *opéra-comique*. Candelabra extend into the orchards and alleyways near the Meander River—the greens and reds of the setting sun. Horatian nymphs in First Empire head-dress—Siberian rondos and Boucher's Chinese ladies.

FAIRY

Pour Hélène se conjurèrent les sèves ornementales dans les ombres vierges et les clartés impassibles dans le silence astral. L'ardeur de l'été fut confiée à des oiseaux muets et l'indolence requise à une barque de deuils sans prix par des anses d'amours morts et de parfums affaissés.

—Après le moment de l'air des bûcheronnes à la rumeur du torrent sous la ruine des bois, de la sonnerie des bestiaux à l'écho des vals, et des cris des steppes.

Pour l'enfance d'Hélène frissonnèrent les fourrures et les ombres—et le sein des pauvres, et les légendes du ciel.

Et ses yeux et sa danse supérieurs encore aux éclats précieux, aux influences froides, au plaisir du décor et de l'heure uniques.

For Helen ornamental sap conspired in astral silence in the virginal darks and the impassive lights. The heat of summer was entrusted to speechless birds and a degree of laziness to a priceless mourning barge drifting through gulfs of dead loves and exhausted perfumes.

—After the time when the woodcutters' wives sang to the sound of the stream in the ruins of the woods, when the bells of the flocks rang out on the hills, and the cries of the steppes.—

For Helen's childhood the furs and shadows shivered—and the hearts of the poor, and the legends of heaven.

And her eyes and her dancing even better than the precious glitter, than the cold influence, than the pleasure of the perfect setting and the perfect moment.

IV

VIE EN VILLE

IV

CITY LIFE

"I want to work in freedom: but in Paris, which I love. Look here, I'm a pedestrian, nothing more; I arrive in the immense city without material resources: but you said to me: Whoever wants to be a worker for fifteen cents a day applies here, does this, lives like that. I apply here, do this, live like that. I beg you to point out jobs that aren't too involving, because thinking takes up large blocks of time. Releasing the poet, these material seesaws become too agreeable. I'm in Paris: I need a *positive economy!*"

Letter to Paul Demeny
(Charleville, August 1871)

Ô cette chaude matinée de février. Le Sud inopportun vint relever nos souvenirs d'indigents absurdes, notre jeune misère.

Henrika avait une jupe de coton à carreau blanc et brun, qui a dû être portée au siècle dernier, un bonnet à rubans, et un foulard de soie. C'était bien plus triste qu'un deuil. Nous faisions un tour dans la banlieue. Le temps était couvert, et ce vent du Sud excitait toutes les vilaines odeurs des jardins ravagés et des prés desséchés.

Cela ne devait pas fatiguer ma femme au même point que moi. Dans une flache laissée par l'inondation du mois précédent à un sentier assez haut, elle me fit remarquer de très petits poissons.

La ville, avec sa fumée et ses bruits de métiers, nous suivait très loin dans les chemins. Ô l'autre monde, l'habitation bénie par le ciel et les ombrages! Le Sud me rappelait les misérables incidents de mon enfance, mes désespoirs d'été, l'horrible quantité de force et de science que le sort a toujours éloignée de moi. Non! nous ne passerons pas l'été dans cet avare pays où nous ne serons jamais que des orphelins fiancés. Je veux que ce bras durci ne traîne plus une *chère image!*

O that warm February morning! The unbothersome South came up here to agitate our ridiculous pauper memories, our youthful poverty.

Henrika had on a brown and white checkered cotton skirt which must have been worn a hundred years ago, a bonnet with ribbons, a silk scarf.It was sadder than a wake. We were taking a walk in the suburbs. The day was overcast, and that wind from the South brought out all the bad smells from the dried-up fields and the gardens gone to pot.

This didn't tire my wife as much as it did me. In a puddle left by the rains of the previous month on quite a high path, she showed me some very tiny fishes.

The city, with its smoke and its factory noises, followed us along the roads pretty far out. O that other world, that dwelling place blessed by sky and shade! The South brought back those miserable memories of childhood, my summertime despairs, the horrible amounts of strength and know-how fate has always robbed me of. No! we won't spend the summer in this avaricious place where we'll never be anything but a couple of love-sick castaways. I want this toughened arm of mine to quit lugging around a *pretty picture!*

Des ciels gris de cristal. Un bizarre dessin de ponts, ceux-ci droits, ceux-là bombés, d'autres descendant ou obliquant en angles sur les premiers, et ces figures se renouvelant dans les autres circuits éclairés du canal, mais tous tellement longs et légers que les rives, chargées de dômes s'abaissent et s'amoindrissent. Quelques-uns de ces ponts sont encore chargés de masures. D'autres soutiennent des mâts, des signaux, de frêles parapets. Des accords mineurs se croisent, et filent, des cordes montent des berges. On distingue une veste rouge, peut-être d'autres costumes et des instruments de musique. sont-ce des airs populaires, des bouts de concerts seigneuriaux, des restants d'hymnes publics? L'eau est grise et bleue, large comme un bras de mer.

Un rayon blanc, tombant du haut du ciel, anéantit cette comédie.

BRIDGES

Skies of gray crystal. A bizarre design of bridges, some straight, some arched, others coming down at oblique angles to the first; and these shapes repeating themselves in other lighted circles of the canal, but all so long and lightweight that the banks, loaded with domes, sink down and shrink. Several of these bridges are still covered with hovels. Others support masts, signals, frail ramparts. The lesser cables crisscross each other and disappear; ropes rise from the shores. You can see a red jacket, possibly other costumes, and musical instruments. Are these popular songs, odds and ends from highflown concerts, leftover public hymns? The water is gray and blue, broad as an arm of the sea.

A white ray, falling from high in the sky, squelches this silly sham.

VILLE

Je suis un éphémère et point trop mécontent citoyen d'une métropole crue moderne parce que tout goût connu a été éludé dans les ameublements et l'extérieur des maisons aussi bien que dans le plan de la ville. Ici vous ne signaleriez les traces d'aucun monument de superstition. La morale et la langue sont réduites à leur plus simple expression, enfin! Ces millions de gens qui n'ont pas besoin de se connaître amènent si pareillement l'éducation, le métier et la vieillesse, que ce cours de vie doit être plusieurs fois moins long que ce qu'une statistique folle trouve pour les peuples du continent. Aussi comme, de ma fenêtre, je vois des spectres nouveaux roulant à travers l'épaisse et éternelle fumée de charbon,—notre ombre des bois, notre nuit d'été!— des Érinnyes nouvelles, devant mon cottage qui est ma patrie et tout mon coeur puisque tout ici ressemble à ceci,—la Mort sans pleurs, notre active fille et servante, un Amour désespéré, et un joli Crime piaulant dans la boue de la rue.

CITY

I'm an ephemeral and not too discontented citizen of a metropolis that's considered modern because all known standards of taste have been side-stepped in the furnishings and outsides of the houses as well as in the layout of the city. You'd have a hard time finding the least sign of any monument to superstition here. Morality and language have been reduced to their simplest expression, at last! These millions of citizens, who haven't the slightest need to know each other, conduct their education, their affairs, and their old age so completely alike that the crazy statistics conclude their life spans can only be several times less long than those of people on the Continent. Likewise, from my window, I watch new ghosts rolling through the thick everlasting coal smoke—our woodsy shade! our summer night!—the latter-day Erinys in front of my cottage which is my country and my whole heart, since everything here looks like this,—Death without tears, our competent girl and servant, a desperate Love, and a pretty Crime whining in the muck of the street.

ORNIÈRES

À droite l'aube d'été éveille les feuilles et les vapeurs et les bruits de coin du parc, et les talus de gauche tiennent dans leur ombre violette les mille rapides ornières de la route humide. Défilé de féeries. En effet: des chars chargés d'animaux de bois doré, de mâts et de toiles bariolées, au grand galop de vingt chevaux de cirque tachetés, et les enfants et les hommes sur leurs bêtes les plus étonnantes;—vingt véhicules, bossés, pavoisés et fleuris comme des carrosses anciens ou de contes, pleins d'enfants attifés pour une pastorale suburbaine.—Même des cercueils sous leur dais de nuit dressant les panaches d'ébène, filant au trot des grandes juments bleues et noires.

RUTS

To the right, summer dawn wakes up the leaves and the mists and the sounds in this corner of the park, and to the left the slopes contain in their purplish shade the thousand swift ruts of the sloshy road. Parade of fairies! Here they come: floats loaded with golden wooden animals, poles and bright-painted posters vibrating to the frenzied gallop of twenty dappled circus horses, and children, and men, on their most fantastic beasts;—twenty embossed wagons decorated with flags and flowers like ancient fairy tale coaches, full of children decked out for an outing in the suburbs.—Even coffins under pitch-dark canopies with jet-black plumes, zooming along to the trot of huge mares, all black and blue.

VILLES I

Ce sont des villes! C'est un peuple pour qui se sont montés ces Alleghanys et ces Libans de rêve! Des chalets de cristal et de bois qui se meuvent sur des rails et des poulies invisibles. Les vieux cratères ceints de colosses et de palmiers de cuivre rugissent mélodieusement dans les feux. Des fêtes amoureuses sonnent sur les canaux pendus derrière les chalets. La chasse des carillons crie dans les gorges. Des corporations de chanteurs géants accourent dans des vêtements et des oriflammes éclatants comme la lumière des cimes. Sur les plates-formes au milieu des gouffres les Rolands sonnent leur bravoure. Sur les passerelles de l'abîme et les toits des auberges l'ardeur du ciel pavoise les mâts. L'écroulement des apothéoses rejoint les champs des hauteurs où les centauresses séraphiques évoluent parmi les avalanches. Au-dessus du niveau des plus hautes crêtes, une mer troublée par la naissance éternelle de Vénus, chargée de flottes orphéoniques et de la rumeur des perles et des conques précieuses,—la mer s'assombrit parfois avec des éclats mortels. Sur les versants des moissons de fleurs grandes comme nos armes et nos coupes, mugissent. Des cortèges de Mabs en robes rousses, opalines, montent des ravines. La-haut, les pieds dans la cascade et les ronces, les cerfs tètent Diane. Les Bacchantes des banlieues sanglotent et la lune brûle et hurle. Vénus entre dans les cavernes des forgerons et des ermites. Des groupes de beffrois chantent les idées des peuples. Des châteaux bâtis en os sort la musique inconnue. Toutes les légendes évoluent et les élans se ruent dans les bourgs. Le paradis des orages s'effondre. Les sauvages dansent sans cesse la fête de la nuit. Et une heure je suis descendu dans le mouvement d'un boulevard de Bagdad où des compagnies ont chanté la joie du travail nouveau, sous une brise épaisse, circulant sans pouvoir éluder les fabuleux fantômes des monts où l'on a dû se retrouver.

Quels bons bras, quelle belle heure me rendront cette région d'où viennent mes sommeils et mes moindres mouvements?

CITIES I

These are cities! This is a people which these dream-Alleghenies and these dream-Lebanons have sprung up for! Bungalows of crystal and wood moving along invisible rails and pulleys. Old craters circled by colossi and copper palm trees roaring with melody among the fires. Love feasts ringing out on the suspended canals behind the bungalows. The sounds of chimes chasing each other in the gulleys. Guilds of gigantic singers coming together in robes and banners as shining as the light on mountain peaks. On scaffoldings among the abysses, Rolands roaring with bravado. On foot-bridges over the depths and roofs of inns, the brightness of the sky decking out the flag-poles. The break-down of apotheoses linking the fields with the heights where seraphic she-centaurs evolve among the avalanches. Above the level of the highest crests, a sea stirred up by the ceaseless birth of Venus, brimming with orphic navies and the roar of pearls and precious shells,—the sea at times grows dark with dying flashes. On the slopes, harvests of flowers as big as our goblets and weapons, howling. Long lines of Mabs in dresses of red and opal climb up the ravines. Further up, stand-ing in waterfalls and blackberries, stags suck Diana's tits. The Bac-chantes of the suburbs sob, and the moon fumes and hoots. Venus walks into the caves of blacksmiths and hermits. Crowds of bell towers ring out the ideas of the people. An unfamiliar music flows out of castles built of bones. All the legends come to a head and all the urges hit the towns. The heaven of rages breaks down. The savages dance non-stop the feast of night. And for a whole hour, I went down into the noisy give-and-take of a boulevard in Bagdad where throngs of com-panions were joyfully celebrating the New Work, in that breezy obscurity, moving ahead but not steering clear of the fabulous phantasms of the mountains, where all had to orient themselves once again.

What strong arms, what beautiful hour will give me back that region from which my sleep and my slightest moves derive?

L'acropole officielle outre les conceptions de la barbarie moderne les plus colossales. Impossible d'exprimer le jour mat produit par ce ciel immuablement gris, l'éclat impérial des bâtisses, et la neige éternelle du sol. On a reproduit dans un goût d'énormité singulier toutes les merveilles classiques de l'architecture. J'assiste à des expositions de peinture dans des locaux vingt fois plus vastes qu'Hampton-Court. Quelle peinture! Un Nabuchodonosor norwégien a fait construire les escaliers des ministères; les subalternes que j'ai pu voir sont déjà plus fiers que des Brahmanes, et j'ai tremblé à l'aspect des gardiens de colosses et officiers de constructions. Par le groupement des bâtiments en squares, cours et terrasses fermées, on a évincé les cochers. Les parcs représentent la nature primitive travaillée par un art superbe. Le haut quartier a des parties inexplicables: un bras de mer, sans bateaux, roule sa nappe de grésil bleu entre des quais chargés de candélabres géants. Un pont court conduit à une poterne immédiatement sous le dôme de la Sainte-Chapelle. Ce dôme est une armature d'acier artistique de quinze mille pieds de diamètre environ.

Sur quelques points des passerelles de cuivre, des plates-formes, des escaliers qui contournent les halles et les piliers, j'ai cru pouvoir juger la profondeur de la ville! C'est le prodige dont je n'ai pu me rendre compte: quels sont les niveaux des autres quartiers sur ou sous l'acropole? Pour l'étranger de notre temps la reconnaissance est impossible. Le quartier commerçant est un circus d'un seul style, avec galeries à arcades. On ne voit pas de boutiques, mais la neige de la chaussée est écrasée; quelques nababs aussi rares que les promeneurs d'un matin de dimanche à Londres, se dirigent vers une diligence de diamants. Quelques divans de velours rouge: on sert des boissons polaires dont le prix varie de huit cents à huit mille roupies. À l'idée de chercher des théâtres sur ce circus, je me réponds que les boutiques doivent contenir des drames assez sombres. Je pense qu'il y a une police. Mais la loi doit être tellement étrange, que je renonce à me faire une idée des aventuriers d'ici.

The official acropolis outdistances the most colossal conceptions of modern barbarism. Impossible to do justice to the flat daylight produced by this immutably gray sky, the imperial glossiness of the buildings, and eternal snow on the ground. With a unique taste for the gigantic, they have reproduced all the classical marvels of architecture, and I visit art exhibits in rooms twenty times the size of Hampton Court. What paintings! A Norwegian Nebuchadnezzar had the stairways of the government buildings built; the second-stringers I met were already haughtier than the Brahmins, and I literally quaked at the sight of the guards of colossi and superintendents of structures. By grouping the buildings in squares, with yards and driveways closed, they're keeping out the cabs. The parks are displays of primitive nature improved with superb artistry, the upper part of town contains things no one can explain: an arm of the sea, with no boats, rolls up its sleet-blue sleeves between piers loaded with gigantic candelabra. A short bridge takes you to the back door right under the dome of the Sainte-Chapelle. This dome is an artistic framework of steel fifteen thousand feet in diameter, roughly.

From certain points on the copper footbridges, on the platforms, on the stairways that spiral up around the markets and the pillars, I thought I might be able to judge the city's depth! This is the marvel I couldn't figure out: What are the levels of the other districts above or beneath the acropolis? For the outsider of our time, recognition's impossible. The business district is a circus built in uniform style, with arcades added. The stores can't be seen, but the snow on the sidewalks is trampled: a few nabobs, as rare as walkers in London on a Sunday morning, are moving toward a diamond stagecoach. A few red velvet divans: ice-cold drinks are served, varying in price from eight hundred to eight thousand rupees. When it occurs to me to look for theaters in this circus, I'm reminded that the stores must be featuring gloomy enough shows. I imagine there's a police force. But the law must be so weird that I give up trying to figure out what adventurers would look like here.

Le faubourg, aussi élégant qu'une belle rue de Paris, est favorisé d'un air de lumière. L'élément démocratique compte quelques cents âmes. Là encore, les maisons ne se suivent pas; le faubourg se perd bizarrement dans la campagne, le «Comté» qui remplit l'occident éternel des forêts et des plantations prodigieuses où les gentilshommes sauvages chassent leurs chroniques sous la lumière qu'on a créée.

In the suburb, as beautiful as an elegant Paris street, the air you breathe is just like light, and the local democratic party numbers a few hundred souls. Here, also, the houses don't follow one another. The suburb loses itself strangely in the country—the "County" filling the everlasting west of the forests and of the fantastic plantations, where savage gentlemen track down their daily news by invented light.

Du détroit d'indigo aux mers d'Ossian, sur le sable rose et orange qu'a lavé le ciel vineux, viennent de monter et de se croiser des boulevards de cristal habités incontinent par de jeunes familles pauvres qui s'alimentent chez les fruitiers. Rien de riche.—La ville!

Du désert de bitume fuient droit en déroute avec les nappes de brumes échelonnées en bandes affreuses au ciel qui se recourbe, se recule et descend, formé de la plus sinistre fumée noire que puisse faire l'Océan en deuil, les casques, les roues, les barques, les croupes.—La bataille!

Lève la tête: ce pont de bois, arqué; les derniers potagers de Samarie; ces masques enluminés sous la lanterne fouettée par la nuit froide;l'ondine niaise à la robe bruyante, au bas de la rivière; ces crânes lumineux dans les plans de pois—et les autres fantasmagories—la campagne.

Des routes bordées de grilles et de murs, contenant à peine leurs bosquets, et les atroces fleurs qu'on appellerait coeurs et soeurs, Damas damnant de langueur,—possessions de féeriques aristocraties ultraRhénanes, Japonaises, Guaranies, propres encore à recevoir la musique des anciens—et il y a des auberges qui pour toujours n'ouvrent déjà plus—il y a des princesses, et si tu n'es pas trop accablé, l'étude des astres—le ciel.

Le matin où avec Elle, vous vous débattîtes parmi les éclats de neige, les lèvres vertes, les glaces, les drapeaux noirs et les rayons bleus, et les parfums pourpres du soleil des pôles,—ta force.

From the indigo straits to Ossian's seas, over the pink and orange sand washed by the winey sky, crystal boulevards have just risen and crossed, settled right away by poor young families who get their groceries at the fruitstands. Nothing expensive.—The city!

From the asphalt desert, helmets, wheels, barges, buttocks, run at break-neck speed with sheets of fog spread out in atrocious strips across a sky that bends back, pulls out and comes down, shaped by the most frightening black smoke the Ocean in mourning can muster.—The battle!

Look upwards: this wooden bridge, arched; these last vegetable gardens from Samaria; these illuminated masks under the lantern whipped by the cold night; the silly water nymph in a noisy dress, down by the river; these luminous skulls in a row of peas—and the other phantasmagoria—the country.

Roads bordered by grillwork and walls that can barely hold back their woods, and the atrocious flowers called hearts and sisters. Damask cursing quietly—possessions of magic aristocracies. Upper-Rhenish, Japanese, Guaranian, still qualified to intercept the music of the ancients—and there are inns that now will never open again—there are princesses and, if you're not too overwhelmed, the study of the stars.—The sky.

That morning with Her, when you fought it out among these flashing snows, these green lips, these icebergs, these black flags and blue beams, and these purple perfumes of the polar sun.—Your strength.

Bien après les jours et les saisons, et les êtres et les pays,

Le pavillon en viande saignante sur la soie des mers et des fleurs arctiques. (Elles n'existent pas.)

Remis des vieilles fanfares d'héroïsme—qui nous attaquent encore le coeur et la tête—loin des anciens assassins.

Oh! Le pavillon en viande saignante sur la soie des mers et des fleurs arctiques. (Elles n'existent pas.)

Douceurs!

Les brasiers, pleuvant aux rafales de givre.—Douceurs!—les feux à la pluie du vent de diamants jetée par le coeur terrestre éternellement carbonisé pour nous.—Ô monde!—

(Loin des vieilles retraites et des vieilles flammes, qu'on entend, qu'on sent.)

Les brasiers et les écumes. La musique, virement des gouffres et choc des glaçons aux astres.

Ô douceurs, ô monde, ô musique! Et là, les formes, les sueurs, les chevelures et les yeux, flottant. Et les larmes blanches, bouillantes,—ô douceurs!—et la voix féminine arrivée au fond des volcans et des grottes arctiques.

Le pavillon...

Long after the days and the seasons, the people and countries,

The flag of bleeding meat on the silk of seas and arctic flowers. (They don't exist.)

Recovered from the old fanfares of heroism—which still assault our hearts and heads—far from the old-time assassins.

Oh the flag of bleeding meat on the silk of seas and arctic flowers. (They don't exist.)

Pleasures!

Live embers, raining down in frosted gusts,—Pleasures!—fires in a rain of diamond-filled wind flung out by the earth's heart everlastingly carbonized for us.—O world!—

(Far from the old hideaways and the old flames we can hear, can feel.)

Fires and foam. Music, whirling of abysses and clacking of icicles against the stars.

O pleasures, O world, O music! And here, the forms, the sweating, the long hair and the eyes, floating. And the white tears, burning—O pleasures!—and the female voice reaching to the depths of volcanoes and arctic dugouts.

The flag. . . .

PROMONTOIRE

L'aube d'or et la soirée frissonnante trouvent notre brick au large en face de cette villa et de ses dépendances, qui forment un promontoire aussi étendu que l'Épire et le Péloponnèse, ou que la grande île du Japon, ou que l'Arabie! Des fanums qu'éclaire la rentrée des théories, d'immenses vues de la défense des côtes modernes; des dunes illustrées de chaudes fleurs et de bacchanales; de grands canaux de Carthage et des Embankments d'une Venise louche, de molles éruptions d'Etnas et des crevasses de fleurs et d'eaux des glaciers, des lavoirs entourés de peupliers d'Allemagne; des talus de parcs singuliers penchant des têtes d'Arbre du Japon; et les façades circulaires de «Royal» ou des «Grand» de Scarbro ou de Brooklyn, et leurs railways flanquent, creusent, surplombent les dispositions dans cet Hôtel, choisies dans l'histoire des plus élégantes et des plus colossales constructions de l'Italie, de l'Amérique et de l'Asie, dont les fenêtres et les terrasses à présent pleines d'éclairages, de boissons et de brises riches, sont ouvertes à l'esprit des voyageurs et des nobles—qui permettent, aux heures du jour, à toutes les tarentelles des côtes,—et même aux ritournelles des vallées illustres de l'art, de décorer merveilleusement les façades du Palais-Promontoire.

Golden dawn and shivering evening find our brig at sea opposite this villa and its dependencies which form a headland as extensive as Epirus and the Peloponnesos, or as the large island of Japan, or as Arabia! Temples lighted up by the return of theories; tremendous views of modern coastal defenses; dunes illuminated by hot flowers and bacchanals; grand canals of Carthage and Embankments of a doubtful Venice; lazy eruptions of Etnas and gullies full of flowers and glacier waters; laundries surrounded by German poplars; strange hilly parks leaning out of the tops of Japanese trees; and circular facades of the "Grands" and the "Royals" of Scarborough and of Brooklyn; and their railways flank, hollow out, and dominate this hotel chosen from among the most elegant and the most colossal buildings of Italy, America, and Asia and whose windows and balconies, now full of illuminations and drinks and heavy breezes, invite the comments of travelers and aristrocrats—who permit, by daylight, all the tarantellas of the coast—and even the ritournellas of the illustrious valleys of Art—to decorate the facades of Headland Palace, marvelously.

V

VIE VISIONNAIRE

V

VISIONARY LIFE

"The poet makes himself a *seer* by a long, immense, and reasoned *derangement of all the senses*. All forms of love, suffering, and madness—he explores himself, he tries out all the poisons on himself and keeps only their quintessences. Unspeakable torture where he really needs faith, all the superhuman strength there is, where he becomes in the midst of everyone else the great sick man, the great criminal, the great condemned—and the supreme Knower!—since he has reached the *unknown!*"

Letter to Paul Demeny
(Charleville, May 1871)

DÉPART

Assez vu. La vision s'est rencontrée à tous les airs.

Assez eu. Rumeurs des villes, le soir, et au soleil, et toujours.

Assez connu. Les arrêts de la vie.—Ô Rumeurs et Visions!

Départ dans l'affection et le bruit neufs!

CUTTING OUT

Seen enough. The vision bumped into, in season and out.

Had enough. Racket of cities, in the evening, and in sunlight, and always.

Known enough. The let-downs of life.—O Rumblings and Visions! Cutting out to affection and new sounds!

Un beau matin, chez un peuple fort doux, un homme et une femme superbes criaient sur la place publique: «Mes amis, je veux qu'elle soit reine!» «Je veux être reine!» Elle riait et tremblait. Il parlait aux amis de révélation, d'épreuve terminée. Ils se pâmaient l'un contre l'autre.

En effet, ils furent rois toute une matinée, où les tentures carminées se relevèrent sur les maisons, et toute l'après-midi, où ils s'avancèrent du côté des jardins de palmes.

One fine morning, in a land of extremely gentle people, a very beautiful man and woman called out, quite loud, in a public place: "Dear friends, I want her to be queen!" "And I want to *be* queen!" She was laughing and trembling. He was telling friends about a revelation, about an ordeal they'd come through. They were weak with happiness.

As a matter of fact, they *were* royalty for a whole morning, while the houses were covered with bright-red bunting, and for a whole afternoon, while they walked in the direction of the palm gardens.

Un coup de ton doigt sur le tambour décharge tous les sons et commence la nouvelle harmonie.

Un pas de tois, c'est la levée des nouveaux hommes et leur en-marche.

Ta tête se détourne:—le nouvel amour! Ta tête se retourne:—le nouvel amour!

«Change nos lots, crible les fléaux, à commencer par le temps», te chantent ces enfants.

«Élève n'importe où la substance de nos fortunes et de nos voeux», on t'en prie.

Arrivée de toujours, qui t'en iras partout.

One tap of your little finger on the drum unleashes all sounds and the new harmony begins!

One step by you and the new men are standing tall and ready to go.

Your head turns one way:—a new kind of love! Your head turns another way:—a new kind of love!

"Change our life, rid us of the plague, start with Time, " these children sing out to you.

"Bring about anywhere at all the reality of good times and wishes come true," they beg you.

Arrived from *all the time,* aboard for *all there is!*

MYSTIQUE

Sur la pente du talus, les anges tournent leurs robes de laine dans les herbages d'acier et d'émeraude.

Des prés de flammes bondissent jusqu'au sommet du mamelon. À gauche le terreau de l'arête est piétiné par tous les homicides et toutes les batailles, et tous les bruits désastreux filent leur courbe. Derrière l'arête de droite la ligne des orients, des progrès.

Et tandis que la bande, en haut du tableau, est formée de la rumeur tournante et bondissante des conques des mers et des nuits humaines,

La douceur fleurie des étoiles et du ciel et du reste descend en face du talus, comme un panier, contre notre face, et fait l'abîme fleurant et bleu là-dessous.

MYSTIC

On the slope of the hill the angels whirl their woolen robes in grasses of steel and emerald.

Meadows of flame leap up to the top of the little hill. On the left, the earth of the ridge has been trampled by all the murder and all the battles, and all the sounds of disaster flare up in their orbit. Behind the ridge on the right , the line of the Orient, of progressions.

And whereas the band, at the top of the picture, is made up of whirling and leaping uproars of seashells and mortal nights,

The flowering sweetness of stars and sky and the rest falls across the slope, like a basket, before our faces, and makes the abyss all flowers and blue beneath.

VEILLÉES

I

C'est le repos éclairé, ni fièvre, ni langueur, sur le lit ou sur le pré.
C'est l'ami ni ardent ni faible. L'ami.
C'est l'aimée ni tourmentante ni tourmentée. L'aimée.
L'air et le monde point cherchés. La vie.
—Était-ce donc ceci?
—Et le rêve fraîchit.

II

L'éclairage revient à l'arbre de bâtisse. Des deux extrémités de la salle, décors quelconques, des élévations harmoniques se joignent. La muraille en face du veilleur est une succession psychologique de coupes de frises, de bandes atmosphériques et d'accidences géologiques.—Rêve intense et rapide de groupes sentimentaux avec des êtres de tous les caractères parmi toutes les apparences.

III

Les lampes et les tapis de la veillée font le bruit des vagues, la nuit, le long de la coque et autour du steerage.
La mer de la veillée, telle que les seins d'Amélie.
Les tapisseries, jusqu'à mi-hauteur, des taillis de dentelle, teinte d'émeraude, où se jettent les tourterelles de la veillée.

———————

La plaque du foyer noir, de réels soleils des grèves: ah! puits des magies; seule vue d'aurore, cette fois.

NIGHT-WATCHES

I

It's time out in the glow, with no fever and no faintness, on a bed or in a field.

It's the buddy with no violence and no weakness. The buddy.

It's the girl friend neither tormentor nor tormented. The girl friend.

Air and a world not striven for. The life.

—Was this really *it?*

—And the dream cooled off.

II

The lighting comes back to the high beam. From the two opposite ends of the room, some decorations, harmonic highs combining. The wall opposite the onlooker is a psychological sequence of breaks, friezes, atmospheric bands, and geological accidents.—Intense, fast-moving dream of emotional groupings with people of all conceivable kinds in the thick of appearances.

III

The lamps and rugs of this watch make the noise of waves, at night, along the keel and around the steerage deck.

The sea of the night-watch, like the titties of Emily.

The tapestries, halfway up, undergrowths of emerald-tainted lace, where the doves of the night-watch fling themselves.

Smutchy back-wall of the fireplace, real suns on real seashores! Ah! wells of magic. Mere glimpse of dawn, that time.

En quelque soir, par exemple, que se trouve le touriste naïf, retiré de nos horreurs économiques, la main d'un maître anime le clavecin des prés; on joue aux cartes au fond de l'étang, miroir évocateur des reines et des mignonnes; on a les saintes, les voiles, et les fils d'harmonie, et les chromatismes légendaires, sur le couchant.

Il frissonne au passage des chasses et des hordes. La comédie goutte sur les tréteaux de gazon. Et l'embarras des pauvres et des faibles sur ces plans stupides!

À sa vision esclave, l'Allemagne s'échafaude vers des lunes; les déserts tartares s'éclairent; les révoltes anciennes grouillent dans le centre du Céleste Empire, par les escaliers et les fauteuils de roc—un petit monde blême et plat, Afrique et Occidents, va s'édifier. Puis un ballet de mers et de nuits connues, une chimie sans valeur, et des mélodies impossibles.

La même magie bourgeoise à tous les points où la malle nous déposera! Le plus élémentaire physicien sent qu'il n'est plus possible de se soumettre à cette atmosphère personnelle, brume de remords physiques, dont la constatation est déjà une affliction.

Non! Le moment de l'étuve, des mers enlevées, des embrasements souterrains, de la planète emportée, et des exterminations conséquentes, certitudes si peu malignement indiquées dans la Bible et par les Normes et qu'il sera donné à l'être sérieux de surveiller.— Cependant ce ne sera point un effet de légende!

HISTORIC EVENING

On some evening, for instance, when the unsophisticated tourist has retired from our economic nightmares, a master's hand makes the harpsichord of the fields come alive; they're playing cards at the bottom of the pool, a mirror which brings to mind a few queens and call-girls; they've got saints, veils, threads of harmony, and legendary ir-ridescence out there in the sunset.

He shivers at the passing of hunts and hordes. Comedy drips onto the stages of grass. And the embarassment of the weak and the poor in these stupid arrangements!

Before his slave-vision, Germany is scaffolding itself toward some moons; Tartar deserts are lighting up; ancient revolts are rumbling in the center of the Celestial Empire; over stairways and armchairs of rock, a pale and flat little world, Africa and Occidents, will be built up. Then a ballet of well-known seas and nights, a worthless chemistry, and impossible melodies.

The same middle-class magic wherever the mail train drops you off! The most elementary physicist feels it's no longer possible to put up with this personalized atmosphere, this smog of physical remorse, which is a headache to even think about.

No! the time of the cauldron, of seas swept aside, of underground fire-storms, of the planet blown away and the resulting exterminations, certainties indicated with so little malice by the Bible and the Nornes and which serious persons would do well to prepare for.—Yet it'll be nothing legends are made of!

MOUVEMENT

Le mouvement de lacet sur la berge des chutes du fleuve,
Le gouffre à l'étambot,
La célérité de la rampe,
L'énorme passade du courant
Mènent par les lumières inouïes
Et la nouveauté chimique
Les voyageurs entourés des trombes du val
Et du strøm.

Ce sont les conquérants du monde
Cherchant la fortune chimique personnelle;
Le sport et le comfort voyagent avec eux;
Ils emmènent l'éducation
Des races, des classes et des bêtes, sur ce vaisseau,
Repos et vertige
À la lumière diluvienne,
Aux terribles soirs d'étude.

Car de la causerie parmi les appareils, le sang, les fleurs, le feu, les
    bijoux,
Des comptes agités à ce bord fuyard,
—On voit, roulant comme une digue au delà de la route hydraulique
    motrice,
Monstrueux, s'éclairant sans fin,—leur stock d'études;
Eux chassés dans l'extase harmonique,
Et l'héroïsme de la découverte.
Aux accidents atmosphériques les plus surprenants,
Un couple de jeunesse s'isole sur l'arche
—Est-ce ancienne sauvagerie qu'on pardonne?—
Et chante et se poste.

MOVEMENT

The rhythmic movement on the river falls' bank,
The whirlpool at the sternpost,
The swiftness of the hand-rail,
And the huge passing of the current
Conduct through unheard-of lights
And a chemical newness
The voyagers surrounded by the waterspouts of the valley
And the strøm.

These are the conquerors of the world
Seeking a personal chemical fortune;
Sports and comforts travel along with them;
They bring the education
Of races, classes, and animals, on this boat,
Repose and vertigo
To this diluvian light,
To terrible nights of study.

Since from the talk among the apparatus, the blood, the flowers,
        the fire, the jewels,
From the agitated counting aboard this fugitive ship,
—You can see, rolling like a dyke beyond the hydraulic power-road,
Monstrous, endlessly illuminated—their stock of studies;
Themselves hunted into harmonic ecstasy,
And the heroism of discovery.
During the most unbelievable incidental transactions,
A young couple moves apart at the bridge
—Is it an ancient savagery that's forgivable?—
And sings and *stands pat.*

Il est l'affection et le présent puisqu'il a fait la maison ouverte à l'hiver écumeux et à la rumeur de l'été, lui qui a purifié les boissons et les aliments, lui qui est le charme des lieux fuyants et le délice sur-humain des stations. Il est l'affection et l'avenir, la force et l'amour que nous, debout dans les rages et les ennuis, nous voyons passer dans le ciel de tempête et les drapeaux d'extase.

Il est l'amour, mesure parfaite et réinventée, raison merveilleuse et imprévue, et l'éternité: machine aimée des qualités fatales. Nous avons tous eu l'épouvante de sa concession et de la nôtre: ô jouissance de notre santé, élan de nos facultés, affection égoïste et passion pour lui, lui qui nous aime pour sa vie infinie…

Et nous nous le rappelons et il voyage… Et si l'Adoration s'en va, sonne, sa promesse sonne: «Arrière ces superstitions, ces anciens corps, ces ménages et ces âges. C'est cette époque-ci qui a sombré!»

Il ne s'en ira pas, il ne redescendra pas d'un ciel, il n'accomplira pas la rédemption des colères de femmes et des gaîtés des hommes et de tout ce Péché: car c'est fait, lui étant, et étant aimé.

Ô ses souffles, ses têtes, ses courses; la terrible célérité de la perfec-tion des formes et de l'action!

Ô fécondité de l'esprit et immensité de l'univers!

Son corps! Le dégagement rêvé, le brisement de la grâce croisée de violence nouvelle!

Sa vue, sa vue! tous les agenouillages anciens et les peines *relevées* à sa suite.

Son jour! l'abolition de toutes souffrances sonores et mouvantes dans la musique plus intense.

Son pas! les migrations plus énormes que les anciennes invasions.

Ô lui et nous! l'orgueil plus bienveillant que les charités perdues.

O monde! et le chant clair des malheurs nouveaux!

Il nous a connus tous et nous a tous aimés. Sachons, cette nuit d'hiver, de cap en cap, du pôle tumultueux au château, de la foule à la plage, de regards en regards, forces et sentiments las, le héler et le voir, et le renvoyer, et sous les marées et au haut des déserts de neige, suivre ses vues, ses souffles, son corps, son jour.

He's feelings and he's now, because he's held open house for the heady blizzards of winter as well as summer-time's easy rap-sessions—he's unpolluted our food and drink—he's the magus of running away and the not-quite-human bliss of standing still. He's feelings and the future, the heart and energy passing overhead between the storms and the streamers of ecstasy, as we stand pat in our boredoms and rages.

He's love, the perfect measure invented from scratch, the marvelous and unthinkable logic, and eternity: the instrument loved for its fatality. We've all known the terror of his allowance and our own: the thrill of good health, the pleasuring of the senses, the ego-centered lust and the wild craving for him—who loves us as long as his life, without end. . . .

And we call him to mind and he's traveling. . . . And if Adoration goes, rings, his promise rings: "Down with these superstitions, these wrinkled bodies, these couples and old ages. It's this age that's failed!"

He won't go away, won't come down again from some heaven, won't fulfill the redemption of women's furies nor the gaieties of men nor of all this Sin: it's already done, since he *is* and he's loved.

O his breaths, his heads, his races: the tremendous swiftness of flawless forms and action!

O inventiveness of the mind and fullness of the universe!

His body! the dreamed-of liberation, the thrashing of loveliness matched with new violence!

The sight of him, the sight! and the old boot-licking and the penalties null and void when he comes.

His day! the abolition of all blatant and restless sufferings in music more intense.

His step! migrations more far-ranging than the invasions of early times.

O he and us! pride more largehearted than lost charities.

O world! and the clear sounds of up-to-date adversities.

He's known all of us and has loved us all: let's, this winter night, from Cape to Cape, from the uproarious pole to the castle, from the crowd to the beach, from look to look, our energies at low ebb, announce him and see him, and send him on his way, and down under tides and high in deserts of snow, go after his sight—his breath—his body—his day—

À ma soeur Louise Vanaen de Voringhem:—Sa cornette bleue tournée à la mer du Nord.—Pour les naufragés.

À ma soeur Léonie Aubois d'Ashby. Baou!—l'herbe d'été bourdonnante et puante.—Pour la fièvre des mères et des enfants.

À Lulu,—démon—qui a conservé un goût pour les oratoires du temps des Amies et de son éducation incomplète.—Pour les hommes! À madame ***.

À l'adolescent que je fus. À ce saint vieillard, ermitage ou mission.

À l'esprit des pauvres. Et à un très haut clergé.

Aussi bien à tout culte en telle place de culte mémoriale et parmi tels événements qu'il faille se rendre, suivant les aspirations du moment ou bien notre propre vice sérieux.

Ce soir, à Circeto des hautes glaces, grasse comme le poisson, et enluminée comme les dix mois de la nuit rouge,—(son coeur ambre et spunk),—pour ma seule prière muette comme ces régions de nuit et précédant des bravoures plus violentes que ce chaos polaire.

À tout prix et avec tous les airs, même dans des voyages métaphysiques.—Mais plus *alors*.

To Sister Louise Vanaen de Voringhem:—Her blue coif turned toward the North Sea.—Pray for the ship-wrecked.

To Sister Leonie Aubois d'Ashby, woof!—the buzzing, stinking summer grass.—Pray for the fever of mothers and children.

To Lulu—devil—who has retained a taste for oratories of the time of the Friends and her unfinished education.—Pray for the men. To Madame***.

To the adolescent I once was. To that holy old man, hermitage or mission.

To the spirit of the poor. And to an extremely high clergy.

As well as to all cults in every place of traditional worship and to whatever events one must take part in according to the aspirations of the moment or else to one's own serious vice.

This evening, to Cicerto of the lofty ices, fat as fish, and illuminated like the ten months of the scarlet night—(her heart amber and spunky)—for my only prayer silent like these regions of night, and coming before bravuras more violent than this polar chaos.

At all costs, in season and out, even in metaphysical journeys.—But no more *then*.

SOLDE

À vendre ce que les Juifs n'ont pas vendu, ce que noblesse ni crime n'ont goûté, ce qu'ignorent l'amour maudit et la probité infernale des masses; ce que le temps ni la science n'ont pas à reconnaître;

Les Voix reconstituées; l'éveil fraternel de toutes les énergies chorales et orchestrales et leurs applications instantanées; l'occasion, unique, de dégager nos sens!

À vendre les Corps sans prix, hors de toute race, de tout monde, de tout sexe, de toute descendance! Les richesses jaillissant à chaque démarche! Solde de diamants sans contrôle!

À vendre l'anarchie pour les masses; la satisfaction irrépressible pour les amateurs supérieurs; la mort atroce pour les fidèles et les amants!

À vendre les habitations et les migrations, sports, féeries et comforts parfaits, et le bruit, le mouvement et l'avenir qu'ils font!

À vendre les applications de calcul et les sauts d'harmonie inouïs. Les trouvailles et les termes non soupçonnés, possession immédiate,

Élan insensé et infini aux splendeurs invisibles, aux délices insensibles,—et ses secrets affolants pour chaque vice—et sa gaîté effrayante pour la foule.

À vendre les Corps, les voix, l'immense opulence inquestionable, ce qu'on ne vendra jamais. Les vendeurs ne sont pas à bout de solde! Les voyageurs n'ont pas à rendre leur commission de si tôt!

For sale, what the Jews weren't able to sell, what even the upper crust and the gangsters have never been treated to, what's not known in the most repulsive of sexual practices or in the most damnable uprightness of the masses; what neither Time nor Science need give their seal of approval to—:

Re-serviced Voices: the fraternal awakening of all choral and instrumental energies and their immediate putting to use—a once-in-a-lifetime opportunity to free our senses!

For sale, priceless Bodies, without regard to race, world, breed, or sex! Bargains galore in all departments! Unrestricted sale of diamonds!

For sale, anarchy for the masses; satisfaction guaranteed to those who know the score; *unbeatable* deaths for steady customers and lovers.

For sale, homes and migrations, sports, fairylands, and perfect comfort, with all the noise, the movement, and the future that go with them!

For sale, shipments of calculations and truly remarkable harmonic progressions. Discoveries and terminologies undreamed of. Immediate delivery.

Wild, round-the-clock in-rushes to invisible splendors, to intangible delights—with delirious secrets for all the vices—and terrifying gaiety for the in-rushing crowds.

For sale, the Bodies, the voices, the immense and unquestionable opulence, what can never be sold out. The vendors have barely begun to touch this stock! The salesmen needn't rush their orders too soon.

TRANSLATOR'S POSTSCRIPT

— 1 —

Rimbaud's *Illuminations* is one of the most powerfully influential masterpieces of our era, yet no one knows to this day what the exact sequence of its 42 poems should be. The standard French edition, published by Gallimard, follows the order recommended by Rimbaud's friend and fellow-vagabond, Paul Verlaine. But the messy bundle of manuscripts that Rimbaud turned over to Verlaine in Stuttgart in 1875, right after Rimbaud had decided to give up poetry for good, was unedited, uncorrected, unfinished. Verlaine didn't really know what ultimate design Rimbaud had in mind for *Illuminations*. And even though he could have written to the world-wandering Rimbaud in later years to find out, he never did. By the time *Illuminations* was first published in the French magazine *La Vogue,* in 1886, more than ten years had gone by since Rimbaud had stopped writing poems. In his frenetic eagerness to "escape from poetry," Rimbaud had already enlisted in the Dutch colonial army in Batavia and deserted, joined a grubby circus headed for Scandanavia in Hamburg, crossed the Alps on foot and nearly froze to death in a violent snowstorm, worked as a builder's foreman in Cyprus during a summer of record-breaking heat, and had worn himself out as a trader in the hell-holes of Aden and Harar in North Africa (coffee, gum, ivory, hides, guns). When this dying dromomaniac returned to Europe at the age of 37, he completely cut himself off from literary circles. His fans in Paris were calling him "the late Arthur Rimbaud," believing he had died in Abyssinia a few years earlier. At the end, one man—his physician, Dr.Beaudier, who knew about Rimbaud's growing fame in Paris and the numberless enigmas surrounding his work—tried to ask the poet a few questions. But Rimbaud wouldn't talk. As he tormentedly inched his way towards death on the farm of his miserly mother in Roche near Charleville (his cancerous right leg amputated, his left knee hideously swollen from the effects of carcinoma, his whole body tortured by ceaseless insomnia and fever), Rimbaud snapped back at the doctor: "Please cut it out! I'm *through* with all that stuff."

The sequence of the *Illuminations* isn't the only thing Verlaine got wrong. His brief note, accompanying the first publication of these incandescent prose poems, insists that Rimbaud got the idea for his title from some illuminated medieval manuscripts which they had examined together at the British Museum during their London trip in 1872. This preposterously one-sided notion has been repeated too often and has caused generations of Rimbaud's readers to miss the poems' crucially *magical* dimension. Verlaine's biographers have had a harder time than most because of their subject's notoriously bad memory, but by 1886 (they all agree to this) the brain of "pauvre Lélian" was quite completely befuddled with guilt and absinthe. Verlaine had by now forgotten the dream he had once dreamed with the young "voyant" in squalid rented rooms "full of dirty daylight and spider noises" where, with the savage assertiveness of his radiant god-like presence, Rimbaud had outlined his fantastic self-ordained mission to "change life itself" by means of a totally new kind of language, by means of magic. Enid Starkie's researches into the life of Rimbaud have proved conclusively that Rimbaud had made a profound study of occult and illuminist philosophy. We know he had access to the writings of Swedenborg and Eliphas Lévi in his teens. There's evidence that he had devoured such works as Franck's *Histoire de la Kabbale* (1843) and Lévi's *L'Histoire de la Magie* (1860) and *Les Clefs des Grands Mystères* (1861), that he had read and been blasted by Balzac's ecstatic/illuminist novels, *Séraphita* and *Louis Lambert*. His famous "seer letters" of May 1871 are full of illuminist doctrine with its elliptical insolence, full of a terrific thirst for god-like powers. The real poet, he writes to Paul Demeny, "makes himself a *seer* by a long, immense, and reasoned derangement of *all the senses*" in order to become the instrument of higher powers that long to speak through him. The poet can transfigure the drab "real" world into the paradise that shimmers, precariously, right under the skin of mere brute appearance. *This* is what Rimbaud means by "illuminations." An "illuminist" is a person who can transmit light because he enjoys and possesses light himself. Rimbaud knew that occultists have always taken the sun to be the symbol of universal creative energy. Swedenborg says that God appears in the heavens as the sun because he is the Divine Love by which all things of the spirit exist, just as by means of this solar light all natural things exist. When a seer has transformed himself into pure light and has placed his own mortal will in direct touch with the voice-tones of divinity, his words will be magically transmuted into a luminous new kind of language that will change life itself! His powers are now unlimited because he has become one with divinity. He's now a creator in his own right and can control natural forces. He has dominion over birds, fish, flowers, animals, storms, geography, events. The first duty of man, according to Lévi, is to perceive *fully* the significance of what he's able to experience and to *utter* (to "utter" is to "make *out*er"). Then humanity will glow in the dark like the stars and the angels. *That's* the burden Rimbaud was laying on Verlaine in "Vagabonds," one of the most "doctrine"-filled poems in *Illuminations:* "I'd made a vow, in absolute sincerity, to bring him back again to his primitive state of son of the Sun."

— 3 —

A Sunday morning in 1862. Charleville, a provincial French town on the Belgian border. Arthur Rimbaud is 8 years old. The Rimbaud family is setting off for High Mass and the neighbors, knowing what's coming, are poking their heads like clockwork out of the windows, along the way, to gape at this strange procession. First the two little daughters, Vitalie and Isabelle, hand in hand, with their clean white cotton gloves and their shining black buttoned boots. Then the two brothers, Frédéric and Arthur, in their black jackets and slate-blue trousers, their round white collars and their funny little black bowler hats, each carrying a bright blue cotton umbrella. Finally, Madame Rimbaud bringing up the rear—walking alone, in her inflexible dignity, as rigid as a Prussian field-marshall, dressed in blackest black from top to toe, "in mourning" for her "dead" husband who had actually walked out on her one day and was never seen again. Years later, her son would write that when "la mère Rimb" made up her mind it was "like 73 civic administrations wearing pointed leaden helmets." But for the time being, he stifles his curses and wears endless pairs of trousers made of slate-blue material, throughout his school years, because his mother had once bought a huge role of the stuff, cheap, at a clearance sale. She's a tall, thin woman, unbelievably hard and severe—on Sundays, especially—with the gnarled, knotted hands of her peasant father and peasant grandfather before him. A mouth sharp as a knife's edge. A style of terrific authoritarian heaviness that tolerates no backtalk, no contradiction, no appeal. Not a trace of warmth—the type of mother that breeds psychopathic killers, misogynists, and other absolutists. Rimbaud suffered indescribable torments at her hands, as *Illuminations* and *A Season in Hell* both testify, yet like other occultists he envisions a crucial and dignified role for women in the future. In *Histoire de la Magie*, Eliphas Lévi had written: "Woman is the queen of harmony and that is why she must be at the head of the regenerating movement of the future. Woman is higher on the scale of love than man and when love comes to the fore, then woman will be the queen of the universe." Rimbaud openly borrows Lévi's metaphors in "Dawn," "Spells," "Fairyland," "Cities I," but most marvelously in the short poem "Royalty," luminous and flawlessly beautiful. Before starting work on *Illuminations,* he had written to Paul Demeny: "When the endless servitude of woman is smashed, when she lives for and by herself, man—heretofore abominable—having given her her release, she *too* will be a poet! Woman will discover some of the unknown! Will her world of ideas differ from ours? —She will find strange, unfathomable, repulsive, delicious things: we will take them, we will *understand* them." Rimbaud had made up his mind long before Women's Liberation had made it a plank in its platform that both men and women must lose some of their avoirdupois, become light. Light as thunderbolts. "Life's *got* to be changed!"

— 4 —

The language of Rimbaud's *Illuminations* is a very special problem. Everyone recognizes that these strangely glimmerous/hermetic prose poems which Rimbaud wrote before he was 20 years old are absolutely inseparable—along with Nerval's *Les Chimères* and Baudelaire's *Les Fleurs du Mal*—from what's most vital and most exciting in modern French poetry. Rimbaud unquestionably achieved his most astonishing feats of creative originality in the prose poem, a form which he radically re-made to suit his programmatic ambitions. Rimbaud saw himself as a magus violently bent on stripping the mask of falseness off the face of "reality" by stripping language itself of its inherited rhetorical clutter (rhyme, meter, anecdote, description, "content"). To Rimbaud poetry was merely a means to an end, and it's next to impossible to understand Breton, Tzara, Claudel, St.John Perse, and Eluard (not to mention Hart Crane and Henry Miller here in the States) unless one understands this. The *Illuminations* are celebrations of perpetual *amazement* at the incredible brightness of things. Each of the poems is its own verbal universe, its own paradise (the etymology of "paradise" is from *pairi* "around" and *daeẓa* "wall," i.e., an enclosed area, a place completely walled off from all other places). Though certain themes recur in the series—ecstasy, blood, eroticism, anguish, walking, love, gigantism—no single poem really depends on the others or counts on them to achieve its own perfections. Each is intrinsic. (We don't know the exact sequence and we don't *need* to know it.) Each is "inexplicable," each is a miracle of separateness which, paradoxically, is designed to give us a blazing fragment of insight and not the whole picture at once. Occult writers always emphasize the importance of words *in themselves*—their unique shapes, their sounds, their autonomous beauty. All magi believe that the word and its total signification are so completely *one* that if language were effectively used, no explanatory words or clauses would be needed. The single word, perfectly chosen, would be enough to contain all and reveal all (cf."The Aleph" by the Argentinian magus Jorge Luis Borges for a good recent example). Much of the supposed obscurity of Rimbaud's poetry disappears as soon as the reader becomes aware that he's face to face with an awesomely nimble cabalist, a sleight-of-hand artist who can create heavens and hells, or annihilate them, with equal ease. Analogies explain nothing, but perhaps Rimbaud's *Illuminations* can best be understood in terms of an ingenious kaleidoscope. The weirdly contrived phrases and clauses—fragments of colored glass and jewelry, oddments of flesh and nightmare and blood-smeared bone—are carefully arranged by the kaleidoscopist's hand to enchant your eye. But as soon as the entire picture fills the eye-line, a tap of the poet's finger makes everything collapse. Most of the *Illuminations* leave you thus empty-handed and full of amazement. You know you've been struck by lightning, but there's nothing (not even the pieces) left to prove it. One more analogy, perhaps: the pantomimist Marcel Marceau can amaze us by leaning casually, comfortably, on nothing. But Rimbaud, by nature a walker, knows how to take vividly effortless somnambulistic strolls *in mid-air!*

— 5 —

My own ambitions in this completely revised American version of *Iluminations* are: to remain strictly faithful to Rimbaud's anarchist/psychedelic vision of reality; to eliminate a great number of linguistic bloopers and outright distortions that have weakened previous

English renderings of the work; and to construct a long poem that will recreate the terrifying excitements and verbal ingenuities of *Illuminations* in a readable "American idiom" equivalent. I've tried especially hard to find exact American equivalents (exact both in sound and sense) to match the incredible crackle and glow of Rimbaud's "voyou" (hooligan) lingo. Let my translation of "Départ" serve as an illustration. In previous English versions of the poem, the word "départ" in the title and closing line of the original is rendered "departure." Now "departure" is all wrong for Rimbaud. That word's acquired rather formal connotations in English that Rimbaud wouldn't have wanted. A university president or an archbishop might resort to such a word, but not this brilliant little punk/angel with his hair full of lice, with his record for sleeping under more bridges at night than any French poet since François Villon. For us "departure" carries rather restrictive connotations (e.g., the President's "departure" for the summer White House).Or train "departures." Rimbaud could never afford trains and, when he took them, he always tried to bail out before the ticket collector came along. "The man with heels of wind," as Verlaine called him. An obsessional walker. "Cutting out" is the only locution I can think of that has the crispness of the French word and Rimbaud's own slangy bluntness. Other particulars in that poem: "à tous les airs" in the first line is always translated "in all airs," but that's idiomatically a bit ridiculous. What Rimbaud is saying is "in all kinds of weather" or "in season and out." The latter alternative is particularly attractive since there's new evidence that *A Season in Hell* was not in fact Rimbaud's "farewell to literature," that many of the *Illuminations* (perhaps including "Départ") were merely farewells to the kind of descent into horror—or *katábasis*—that he'd been doing in some of the poems he'd written before *Une Saison en Enfer*. In addition, using "season" in the first line preserves the deft alliterations Rimbaud regularly uses in his not-really-prose lines. My "seen" and "season" match his "assez" and "s'est," for instance; my "vision bumped into" and "in season and out" melopoeically approximate his "rencontrée" and "tous les airs." There are hundreds of parallel attempts to reconstruct Rimbaud's subtle and elusive music throughout my versions. (Hopefully, some of them work.) But it's not only their melodic colorlessness that makes earlier versions of *Illuminations* hard to take. Their impossible diction and word choices often date them, also. They characteristically use words like "promontory" instead of "headland," "subsided" instead of "simmered down," "beauteous" instead of "beautiful," "dispersed" instead of "scattered," etc. They tend to opt for the mandarin level of usage, whereas Rimbaud himself has been the inspiration of French poets from Verlaine to Francis Ponge for the delight he takes in the direct, the scatalogical, the *gutsy.*

— 6 —

English and American translators of *Illuminations* have been culpably timid in dealing with Rimbaud's special brand of coarseness. His hellish bad luck in life left deep wounds in his language and these must be retained in the language of the translator if American readers are to understand the view of "heaven" the poet offers. (Rimbaud is known to have been raped, brutally, by tobacco-chewing National Guardsmen during the Paris Commune of 1872.) The poem "Side Show" dramatizes Rimbaud's pederastic nightmare in a ferociously direct way, despite the teasing and obscurantism. The rank smell of sodomy penetrates even the most innocent "descriptive" phrasings in the poem. The last sentence of Rimbaud's first paragraph reads: "On les envoie prendre du dos en ville, affublés d'un luxe dégoûtant." The French argot "prendre du dos" means, quite simply, " to bugger, to fuck in the ass"—and it's quite obvious from the context that a violent homoeroticism between men is involved. Yet Louise Varèse translates this: "They are *sent snaring* in the town, tricked out with nauseating luxury." Wallace Fowlie elegantly shirks the whole thing by rendering it: "They are *sent to the city for trade,* decked out in disgusting finery." What Rimbaud is *really* saying is: "They send these studs to town *to bugger,* decked out in disgusting clothes." Another poem in which Varèse and Fowlie are cautious to the point of blurriness is "H." This is a poem about Rimbaud's masturbation fantasies—he was an 18- or 19-year old kid whose sexual experience had been limited, and Hortense gives him great pleasure and great guilt. The closing words of the poem make it clear that Rimbaud is inviting "discovery" of his sin (and of the secret of his poetic inventiveness) by turning the whole thing, abruptly, into a guessing game, a charade. But much of the poignancy of Rimbaud's (admittedly "mystifying") poem is lost in the soft, almost Victorian wording of the Varèse and Fowlie translations. One feels a need to give back to Rimbaud, in English, the cutting edge of his own "hard" French. There's an uncannily prophetic quality to some of the political poems in *Illuminations,* also, which ought to be brought out for present-day readers in an updated translation. "Democracy," for instance. It sounds as if Rimbaud is describing Vietnam and the events of 1967-68 in the American ghettos, doesn't it? Look again. The poem was prompted by the Franco-Prussian debacle of 1871! ("The seer-poet knows the meaning of the past, the present, and the future," Eliphas Lévi said in *Histoire de la Magie.* "The secret of the resurrection of the dead and the keys of immortality are in his hands. . . . When a great genius prophesies, he is only in reality remembering a sensation he has experienced, for the future is in the past, the past is in the future, and everything is in him.") Another of these "prophetic" poems is "Turned-On Morning," which Rimbaud calls "Matinée d'Ivresse" but which Varese and Fowlie give us as "Morning of Drunkenness," despite the smell of hashish that hovers over the whole poem. Look at the closing line: "Now's the time of the ASSASSINS." The word "assassin" is derived from "hashishin," a smoker of hash, and Rimbaud (who was smoking hash in the early 1870's) was fully aware of this. This poem describes Rimbaud's feelings of anguished disillusionment in the wake of the failure of the Paris Commune, in which he'd probably taken part. His feelings of solidarity with the Paris proletariat were intense (cf."Workers") and the crushing of the Commune by the reactionaries was one of the great death-blows to his spirit. At the peak of his involement in the Commune, he was sure the Revolution (the "New Sound") was here to stay. How accurately "Turned-On Morning" delineates our own nihilistic sense of later betrayals in Chicago (1968) and the numb helpless fury that gripped the brain after the Nixonite "landslide" of 1972, the squelching of the "Revolution" here in the States! But that's neither here nor there. Whether our bodies live or die, Rimbaud's poems are likely to continue to devote their energies to our well-being, night and day—while the ravenous centaurs go on keeping an eye on us from the corner newsstands.

— 7 —

Rimbaud wrote devastatingly about his political and spiritual disappointments in *A Season in Hell,* but worse things were in store for him during the 17 years he had left to live after giving up poetry. He stopped writing but remained an absolutist. His roamings all over the earth are incredible. His death was more nightmarish than anything his own imagination could have invented—pure horror. Here's how the last phase began: In October, 1878, Rimbaud met a man who promised him a job in Egypt if he would go right away to Genoa to take the boat about to leave from there for Alexandria. He traveled the length of France but discovered when he reached Altdorf that the pass across the Alps was closed to traffic for the winter and that, in order to reach Italy, he'd have to cross the mountains on foot. He took off in a violent snowstorm—*on foot!* From Altdorf the road quickly became a wind-lashed labyrinth, rising steeper and steeper. Snowdrifts six feet high often blocked the road, and he had to dig his way through while huge hailstones hit him in the face. There wasn't a shadow to be seen after a long while, no precipices, no mountains, nothing but a blinding white-ness freezing his body, his eyes, his consciousness. He couldn't take his eyes off the blinding whiteness, no matter where he turned. His eye-lashes, eyebrows, moustache were crusted with ice, his ears flayed by the wind, his neck swollen from the effort of climbing. There was noth-ing to help him stick to the road except an occasional telegraph pole (the wires overhead were completely invisible in the all-dazzling whiteness.) At one point in his climb he had to dig his way through a snowdrift three feet deep, along the length of a whole mile. It grew colder and colder as he climbed higher and higher, and he stumbled up-ward in a fever of confusion, sinking into snow up to his armpits. Sud-denly, when he thought he'd reached the limits of his powers of endurance, he saw a pale shadow at the side of a precipice. He col-lapsed before the door of the *Hospice,* paralyzed with cold. When he managed with difficulty to ring the bell, a snarling ugly young monk opened the door to him and took him to a dirty little room and im-patiently gave him the usual meal: a bowl of soup, some bread and cheese, a glass of wine. A hard mattress and flimsy blanket were then given to him and, in the middle of the night, Rimbaud thought he could hear monks singing hymns of joy at having once again robbed the vari-ous governments that subsidized the place. The next morning, after more bread and cheese, Rimbaud left, not much rested. It was a fine day, the wind had died down, and the mountains were illuminated by the brilliant Alpine sunlight. There was no more climbing now, it was down-mountain all the way. Down and down he jogged till he came to warmer air. Then he saw vineyards and fields, birds and farms and cows. At last he reached Lugano, where he could get a train for Genoa on time to board the boat for Alexandria. He was now no longer the angel-faced boy-poet of 1872. At the age of twenty-four, his hair had turned gray and he wore a bleached frizzy little beard. He looked like a walking corpse—but still restlessly *seeking* something. *Le pélerin de l'absolu jusqu'à la fin, quoi!* Nowadays tourists who visit the temple of

Luxor, near Alexandria, are shown the name 'RIMBAUD' deeply carved in the stone high up on a pillar. Over 100 years have gone by since someone carved that name. No one knows to this day how it got there.

—Bertrand Mathieu

A NOTE ON THE TRANSLATOR

Born in Lewiston, Maine, in 1936, Bertrand Mathieu has taught American literature in the U.S., France, Germany, the People's Republic of China, and the Kingdom of Saudi Arabia. He has been twice Fulbright Professor of American Literature, the first time at the University of Athens, Greece, from 1979 to 1981, and more recently at the University of Dakar, Senegal, in West Africa, from 1986 to 1987.

Mathieu has lived and traveled widely in Germany, Italy, Yugoslavia, Greece, Mexico, Turkey, Hong Kong, Taiwan, and the American Southwest, where he earned a Ph.D. in English at the University of Arizona (Tucson) in 1975. His poems, translations, reviews, and critical essays have appeared in *American Poetry Review, City Lights Anthology, Essays in Arts and Sciences, Chicago Review, Concerning Poetry, Partisan Review, Poetry, The Village Voice, Temenos* (London), *L'Arc* (France), and *The Southeastern Review* (Athens), of which he has been Editor-at-Large. A former Woodrow Wilson Fellow, Mathieu has been the recipient of grants from the National Endowment for the Humanities and the Lilly Foundation at Yale University.

Mathieu's book publications include a volume of poems, *Landscape with Voices* (Delta, 1965), early versions of the Rimbaud masterpieces, *A Season in Hell* (Pomegranate Press, 1977) and *Illuminations* (BOA Editions, 1979), and a mythoanalytical study of Orphism, Rimbaud, and Henry Miller entitled *Orpheus in Brooklyn*. Bertrand Mathieu currently lives in Rimbaud's native Charleville, in the French Ardennes, where he is completing a novel about his experiences in Greece, *Freeing Eurydice*.

BOA EDITIONS, LTD.
NEW AMERICAN TRANSLATIONS SERIES

Vol. 1. *Illuminations*
Poems by Arthur Rimbaud
Translated by Bertrand Mathieu

Vol. 2. *Exaltation of Light*
Poems by Homero Aridjis
Translated by Eliot Weinberger

Vol. 3. *The Whale and Other Uncollected Translations*
Richard Wilbur

Vol. 4. *Beings and Things on Their Own*
Poems by Katerina Anghelaki-Rooke
Translated from the Modern Greek by
The Author and Jackie Willcox

Vol. 5. *Anne Hébert: Selected Poems*
Translated by A. Poulin, Jr.

Vol. 6. *Yannis Ritsos: Selected Poems 1938–1988*
Edited and Translated by
Kimon Friar and Kostas Myrsiades

Vol. 7. *The Flowers of Evil and Paris Spleen*
Poems by Charles Baudelaire
Translated by William H. Crosby

Vol. 8. *A Season in Hell and Illuminations*
Poems by Arthur Rimbaud
Translated by Bertrand Mathieu